HOMEWARD VOYAGE

Homeward Voyage

Reflections on Life Changes

Emilie Griffin

Servant Publications
Ann Arbor, Michigan

All scripture quotations, unless otherwise noted, are taken from *The New Jerusalem Bible* © 1966, 1967, and 1968 by Darton, Longman, & Todd Ltd. and Doubleday & Company, Inc. Used by permission.

Published by Servant Publications
P.O. Box 8617
Ann Arbor, Michigan 48107

Cover design by Paula Murphy, Hile Design & Illustration
Cover photo © 1992 Laramie Photographic
Text design by Diane Bareis

94 95 96 97 98   10 9 8 7 6 5 4 3 2 1

Printed in the United States of America
ISBN 0-89283-853-1

Library of Congress Cataloging-in-Publication Data

Griffin, Emilie.
    Homeward voyage : reflections on life changes / Emilie Griffin
        p. cm.
    Includes bibliographical references.
    ISBN 0-89283-853-1 :
    1. Spiritual life.   2. Aging–Religious aspects–Christianity.
3. Aged–Religious life.   4. Griffin, Emilie–Religion   I. Title.
    BV4580.A2G75   1994
    248.4–dc20   94-16698
                                                        CIP

Dedication

For Lucy, Henry, Sarah

Contents

To the Reader

I AM FIFTY-SEVEN AS I WRITE THIS. My mother, to whom I have always been close, is eighty-one. Because I write about spiritual life I look for spiritual interpretations of what is happening. Yet this looking is not without fear. My mother's increasing charm and frailty are mirrors of my future. My children—Lucy, Henry, and Sarah—have grown up. Their lives are becoming disengaged from mine. My husband and I have been married for thirty years. It is time to consider not so much the life-journey, as the end of that journey. My mother and I seem linked in this; my husband travels with us but follows at a slight distance, like a consort ship. I know that his parents have died; perhaps I think he has already made the passage that we are making.

Something new is happening, starkly different from what has gone before. It is time to cut loose from what mattered up to now. We are nearing the end of the journey. It is a winter voyage.

We have settled, figuratively at least, into our deck chairs; we have pulled the blankets up against cold and the ocean spray.

Ours is a reading from the Book of Wisdom:

Or someone else, taking ship to cross the raging sea,
invokes a log even frailer than the vessel that bears him.
No doubt that ship is the product of a craving for gain,
its building embodies the wisdom of the shipwright,

but your providence, Father, is what steers it,
you have opened a pathway even through the sea,
a safe way over the waves,
showing that you can save, whatever happens,
so that even without skill a man may sail abroad.

It is not your will that the works of your Wisdom lie idle,
and hence men entrust their lives to the smallest piece of wood,
cross the high seas on a raft and come safe to port.
Why, in the beginning even,
    while the proud giants were perishing,
the hope of the world took refuge on a raft
and, steered by your hand, preserved the germ of a new
    generation for the ages to come.[1]

I write these thoughts not as instruction, nor as analysis, but
rather as a form of coming to terms with my own history and my
future, in hopes that others will also be strengthened for the
journey.

Emilie Griffin
March, 1994

CHAPTER ONE

Setting Out

WE DO NOT SET OUT TO BECOME OLD. Far from it. We hardly intend even to become middle-aged. Instead we plan to live in some eternal *now* which will lead on to something better, something more complete than what we had before. This movement from present to future is a sequence that can hardly be orchestrated. Instead it has to be lived. Cultivating simplicity, we confront the mystery of how things happen, of actual occasions, droplets of time and experience flowing past the sides of the ship as we knife forward into dark seas, seas without a map. We stand at the bow and feel the lurch and the swell. The sea is in our faces. We move, not knowing how, from one zone to the next.

Sometime in our spiritual travels, as a complete surprise, we notice it has become winter. The waves crashing over the deck are icy cold and gray. For the first time we know are not going to *become* old; we are, without perhaps fully admitting it, already old. Youth and middle age are behind us. This change has occurred, it seems, without preparation, without fair warning.

My friend John Chase was a humorist. "The reason why I'm not doing so well at being old," he said in his eighty-fifth year, "is that I don't have any practice."

But haven't we been preparing all along? Haven't our lives up to now given us some kind of practice?

The people I first loved were old. Their faces were creased and lined, crisscrossed by cobwebs of experience. Even so, they were mostly merry. My grandmother's eyes were brown; her style was mischievous. My grand-aunt, her younger sister, who was almost as close to me, had eyes of china blue. Gray-haired when I first knew them, they gradually went white. A dignity, there from the first, grew sharper and more definite. What I remember most about them, however, was laughter.

So in the daily round of childhood, the routines of mornings and evenings, my grandmother Lucy and her sister Eula became my evening stars, my bright example of being old at its best. I *thought* they were old. In fact, they were women in their early sixties then. They were able-bodied, energetic, vigorous. Yet they were people of a time gone by. They could remember how things had been once, in some former era I longed to hear about. They were charmers, spellbinders, storytellers. I loved to hear them talk, and their talk was always intermingled with a kind of prayer. They were the ones who taught me to pray, intertwining prayer and storytelling at bedtime, in a way so enjoyable I hardly ever wanted it to end. But more than that, they taught me prayer by example. Each morning they devoted time to Bible reading; at any time in their conversation, it seemed, a Bible saying could slip naturally in.

My mother went out to work. Along with my father, she was one of the breadwinners. My grandmother Lucy, whom I called Nui, was my primary caretaker for that reason, the one who was there when I fell or scraped myself or got in trouble somehow. A great intimacy came about because she was always there. Eula, who lived just a few blocks away, taught me to read when I was too young for school. Eula was a schoolteacher who believed in early reading. She herself had learned to read at age four, bored because her older sisters and brother were at school. While her mother did the mending and handwork, Eula sat nearby, coaxing her mother to teach her the alphabet and scrawling the letters with a piece of slate. She was determined! Because Eula opened the world of reading to me, and the world of spiritual life, she became a lifelong friend.

What literary people they were! I remember how much both Nui and Eula loved nursery rhymes and loved to read them with me. It was part of the Englishness of my growing up, part of a link with the past, with generations of people handing things down (thimbles, traditions, family stories, customs, loyalties, ideals). I remember sitting next to Eula on her upstairs porch, flooded with love and sunshine. She taught me how verses galumphed; she made it exciting to read. I vividly remember certain moments: wicker porch chairs with their chintz-covered cushions; frosty glasses of root beer; a china sugar bowl shaped like a pig; Dick and Jane seeing Spot run. I remember straining to form words in my mind; I remember breakthroughs, light dawning. Many years later I saw it all again, as my own children learned to read, small faces bending close to the page, frowning to work out words from baffling letter-squiggles. Most of all I remember the triumph, the joy: Eula's, my children's, my own. Learning to read set us loose on an adventure of mind and heart.

Still another white-haired figure was my cousin Lalita Tenney. Lalita was a nurse! And she was exotic, foreign, having been born in Belize. Lalita spoke English with a Spanish accent. I am told she took care of me when I was an infant in Touro Hospital where I was born. I don't remember that. What I do remember is that she nursed me through pneumonia when I was hospitalized at age nine.

I remember clouds of moisture on the plastic walls of my oxygen tent, sealing me away from the world. I remember the fear. I remember taking penicillin (an experimental drug in those days) around the clock. Also I remember Lalita's golden smile, breaking over me like morning. Around her cheerful face was an aureole of white hair under her starched white nurse's cap. When I grew old, I wanted to look just like her.

So began my fascination with old age; and the fascination grew. I spent many hours with my older relatives: long enough to notice that old men colored their hair with funny-looking tints; long enough to notice the tight, artificial blue-gray curls that old women wore home from the beauty parlor; long enough to notice eccentricities, little lapses of memory ("Now, where did I put my glasses?" "Wasn't my shopping list right on this table?" "Let me see, what was it I came in here for?").

Perhaps not every child is so surrounded with grandmothering and grandfathering figures. (Among the grandfathering figures I have a sudden vivid picture of my paternal grandfather, E.G., dapper in his straw hat, three-piece suit, and high-top shoes; and Eula's husband, Oscar, a university economics professor, generally at work among his books or deep into the newspaper.)

I was an only child, bookish, thought to be gifted, often lonely. I learned to amuse myself with crayons and paper, with modeling clay and blocks, with books most of all. I loved old places and the formality of the past. Often, because my mother worked, and was, for much of my childhood, a single parent, she took me with her to places where she was on assignment. In this way I became the one child most in attendance at meetings of the Louisiana Historical Society, where almost everyone was old.

The meetings were held at the Cabildo, one of the historic government buildings of New Orleans, beside the St. Louis Cathedral near Jackson Square. In the Sala Capitular, where the society often met, the Louisiana Purchase had been signed. In an adjoining room was a death-mask of Napoleon, and the walls were lined with portraits of the early Spanish governors of Louisiana.

To me, the building and the society's members both seemed ancient. The Cabildo's staircase with its wide steps was sinking into the soft Louisiana earth. The structure seemed none too secure, it smelled of mildew and the past. Child of the imagination that I was, I loved it all. In this place I could walk into some by-gone time. Raised in the English tradition, I was drawn by the French and Spanish past, dazzled by flags hanging high in the old cathedral. Here it was possible, like children in story books, to travel back in time.

So, in this way, I came to cherish old age. To me, older people were bearers of a colorful past, heirs to the customs of another age. Mrs. Henry Landry de Freneuse I remember as my earliest example of what it was to be Creole. I remember her in formal black dresses, wearing a lace mantilla, a fringed Spanish shawl, pearl-decorated combs, using a fan. Later, when I discovered Jean Giradoux's play, "The Madwoman of Chaillot," I knew that I had met his madwoman and her cohorts before. It was at the Louisiana Historical Society.

Perhaps the most glamorous event of all was the gala banquet held on the evening of January eighth each year at Antoine's Restaurant to celebrate the American victory at the Battle of New Orleans in 1815. In those days, few children attended this formal affair; I was one of them. It was hard to stay awake through the long-winded formal speeches with their endless repetition of the well-known facts about the Battle. But I loved the ceremony, the formal dress with decorations, the Spanish and French national anthems played by string ensembles. I felt that I was at the center of an ancient, noble, and cosmopolitan culture. Everyone there except my mother and me and one or two others was honorably, visibly old. So in my storybook way I fell in love with old age, in the same way that I seem to fall for lost causes and forgotten heroines.

The old have secrets to tell us, if we only could learn to listen. Children and the old have something in common. God is very fond of them! They are in possession of secret codes to the meanings of existence. Children and the very old are in cahoots; they are in league. That is why (no doubt you have noticed) they get on very well.

When I was nineteen I played an old lady on the stage. I was

Mrs. Hardcastle in a college production of the eighteenth-century comedy, Oliver Goldsmith's *She Stoops to Conquer.* I loved acting; but more than that, I loved becoming old in my imagination. I moved easily into Mrs. Hardcastle's vanity, her gossipy ways, her badgering, her ridiculous flirtations. I learned how to punctuate her funniest remarks with a flutter of her outrageously large fan; I learned how to settle onto a bench with arthritic discomfort and ill ease. Mere slip of a girl that I was, I enjoyed becoming old.

I remember being made up for the role and seeing the lines traced onto my face by an expert make-up man. He explained to me as he did so where the shadows should fall and how the muscles of the face would change as they grew old. I smiled at him while he educated me. (He is gone now to that other place; those are pearls that were his eyes. Does he remember that time we spent together, that exchange of words, that joy in the making of an illusion, the development of a role?)

However much we flirt with it, teasing and pretending our way through such a life-change, we do not in reality want to *be* old. Yet we know our future is calling to us. I remember thinking (when the time came) what a grand old lady I would be; I coveted the beauty of old age; what I wanted was the peace, the charm, the wisdom, the surrender that certain old people seemed to possess.

We know our future is calling. Our future is to be old. Every day leads us relentlessly into an unknown. We are moving on uncharted seas. As believers, we think our faith should strengthen us for the voyage. But does it? Does faith make things as easy as all that? Are we sure that we really approve of the way God has arranged things? Do we really care for the plan? Do we wish the Lord had consulted us beforehand, or given us some way to compromise? We are afraid that they will come for us as they did for Peter and lead us where we do not want to go.

Yet in the faces of the gracious old, a kind transparency attracts us and leads us on. In the loving faces of the old who are at peace with themselves and what they have done, who live each day drenched in grace, we see the possibility of our own transformation, of what we may become. We long to be not only old but good and old, with the cup of long life, life well lived, running over and falling into our laps. How will we find this rare grace, this beauty of many days?

CHAPTER TWO

Memory Travels
with Us

"A woman with shorn white hair is standing at the kitchen window," Truman Capote writes in his story, *A Christmas Memory*. "She is wearing tennis shoes and a shapeless gray sweater over a summery calico dress." Capote is writing out of the well-springs of his own memory. This is Sook, his distant cousin, with whom he lived as a small child. There is a deep bond between them, the bond of their parallel vulnerabilities. "She is small and sprightly, like a bantam hen; but, due to a long, youthful illness, her shoulders are pitifully hunched." Her face, Capote remembers, is craggy as Lincoln's, sun-tinted, delicate, finely boned, her eyes sherry-colored and shy. "We are each other's best friend. She calls me Buddy, in memory of a boy who was formerly her best friend. The other Buddy died in the 1880s when she was still a child."[1] But Capote insists that even now, at sixty-something, Sook is still a child. That is the source of the closeness between them.

I recognize my own experience in Capote's story. When I was a child I had such friends: people who were old and because of their vulnerability, children. Wasn't it also because of their spirituality, their closeness to the Lord, that they were children? They taught me to love God; they taught me how to remain a child always.

When I was twenty-seven I wrote a play in which the best-drawn, perhaps the most sympathetic figure was a woman of eighty. The play concerned a New Orleans Creole family and its tragic determination to found a dynasty. The woman's name was Odile.

"I'm eighty," she says in the first scene. "My face is a cobweb and my hair is spun glass and I take smaller steps than I used to. But I can see clear. I can see far."[2]

When we are young, we think that the old can look directly into the future, into the face of God. As we become older we understand how sometimes God hides his gaze, and as we come closer to the end of our lives we love the things of this life more and more.

Three rain-drenched sparrows in a tree shake themselves loose from the rain. A water-logged hibiscus nods its pink face in our direction. Crepe myrtle trees let their passions run riot through the streets. A splendid sun melts on the river, the silhouette of the city stands against the dawn. Wetness on the windows trembles after the rain. Ivy creeps over the balconies. Babies stir, giggle, and fret in people's arms. Books of faded photographs stand open, revealing memories.

I see clearly now that I have to make a deeper commitment to God, offering him not a day, a week, a season, but everything that I am. It is time to work out tough questions. I understand there are some things in our relationship that I have been avoiding. These are issues I've glossed over, knotty problems I have run away from, hurts I can't handle. It is not as though I were asked to clear a space in my calendar; no. It is God's calendar, not mine. Time is the issue, as it has always been.

Now the irony hits me of that ridiculous expression, "If you can spare the time." Am I really willing to work God into the schedule? Haven't I been trying to exclude him all along? In other times I thought I could sequester a season for the Lord. I thought I could work him into a kind of on-going vacation, a day-to-day retreat in the midst of everything. Now I look back at this visiting with the Lord and see it as superficial: holding conversations with the Lord on crowded beaches where volleyball games are kicking up sand; keeping the encounter going on city streets where the heat is blazing and children are running through sprinklers. I question suddenly the whole idea of retreat: not one part of my life but all of it has to be secluded and put into God's hands.

Do I want to pour myself out and be empty for him? This plunge into simplicity is not only by a change of place but by a shift of attitude, a difference of the heart.

FAITH AND WISDOM

Erik Erikson's work on old age is heartening from the viewpoint of belief. Erikson designs a ladder, a map of what he calls the psychosocial crises. Infancy's crisis is basic trust versus basic mistrust, and its prevailing value is hope. Early childhood opposes autonomy to shame and doubt; its primary value, Erikson says, is will. In the third stage, which Erikson calls the age of play, initiative is in tension with guilt. The guiding value is purpose. At school age, competence begins to surge: industry is in contrast with inferiority. In adolescence, identity is the dominant issue. Fidelity is the call. Young adulthood is governed by the issue of love; intimacy is in tension with isolation. Adulthood contrasts the generative and creative values with stagnation, idling, deterioration. The principal value, as Erikson sees it, is care. At last old age comes, and wisdom is its goal. For Erikson integrity is at odds with disgust and despair.

Erikson starts out from a scientific, not a religious premise. He is somewhat surprised when religion springs up as part of his investigations. "More specifically, if developmental considerations lead us to speak of *hope, fidelity* and *care* as the human strengths or ego qualities emerging from such strategic stages as infancy, adolescence, and adulthood, it should not surprise us (though it did when we became aware of it) that they correspond to such major creedal values as *hope, faith*, and *charity*."[3]

Writing in the eighties (his own eighties, and the 1980's) Erikson is conscious of new patterns in society that are creating a transitional group of "elderlies" who don't conform to historic conceptions of old age. These are the fit, active, "mature persons" we are coming now to recognize on every street corner in the Western world. "On the other hand, should historical changes dissuade us from what we have once perceived old age to be, in our own lifetime and according to the distilled knowledge that has survived in folk wit as well as folk wisdom?"

Erikson says that the role of old age "needs to be re-observed, rethought. To do this he retraces his scheme of life and the values that shape each critical transition. "And as we ascend to the empty square in the upper left corner, we realize that up there we need a word for the last possible form of hope as matured along the whole first ascending vertical."[4] Erikson says the word that suggests itself is *faith*.

Such a scandalous word, it seems, is so unscientific, so primitive, so controversial, that Erikson cannot bring himself to say he suggests the word. He does not propose it, no. Instead, the word "suggests itself"!

Erikson's observation that the word faith suggests itself is consonant with my own notion that for the twentieth century, faith must be reinvented. What we thought was faith may have failed us; but faith is vital to our lives; to believe in God, we must discover him for ourselves, in ways that flow from our real convictions, from our genuine experience.

Erikson is finding out what we as people of faith already knew!
What our Scriptures and our heritage of faith have told us, namely,
that wisdom is childlike trust in the power and plan of God, a
power higher than our own.

Integrity, then, is the mood of the last phase, the winter voyage.
It is time to draw all our experiences together into a schematic
whole, to rest content in who we are and what we have done, to
forgive ourselves for what we haven't done.

Wisdom is more precious than rubies. All the things we desire
can't be compared to her. Length of days is in her right hand, and
in her left hand riches and honor. Her ways are ways of pleasant-
ness, and all her paths are peace. She is a tree of life to them that
lay hold on her; happy is everyone that retains her.

Scripture promises that if we have wisdom, when we lie down,
we won't be afraid. We will lie down and our sleep will be sweet.[5]

LIVING IN THE PRESENT

The winter voyage is a journey not of my own volition, not of
my own design. I, who have difficulty slowing down, I who hurtle
and rush with over-commitment, justifying my work as God's
work, am now brought to a halt. But this halt, this full stop, is not
peaceful, not until I can bring my full acceptance to it. Now I see
myself as a fraud, wanting to be a peacemaker, yet stretched to the
limit by my own anxiety. It is hard to lead others towards balance
and serenity when moving along at white heat and with blazing
intensity. In this halting, in this work-stoppage (which is not a cessation of work but a conversion to a different kind of service), I
recognize the baffling fact of the Lord's supremacy, my own
inability to accept the zig-zag path. If I talk prayer, think prayer,
but don't live it, who am I? What will I become? Is it possible, in
this new predicament, to rest in him? Can I take him again at his
word? "Come to me, all you who labor and are overburdened,
and I will give you rest."[6]

Do I trust the Lord to guide us into a far country? Am I willing to travel with him in a childlike way, not giving much thought to yesterday or tomorrow, concentrating instead on the Lord totally present with me? "Set your hearts on his kingdom first.... do not worry about tomorrow...."[7] Can I let him speak to me in the ocean sounds and the sea gulls' noise? Will I let the sea and stars make me into a child again? "For the one who asks always receives; the one who searches always finds."[8]

Can I stay with God in this nowhere and everywhere? Can I hold on to his closeness and friendship? Just ahead, I see the oncoming tide. Will I have the strength to deal with the next wave? There is something in me that longs for comfort, consolation, sustaining times of intimacy with God. Sometimes, only sometimes, I have these. At other times I feel alienated, drained. God is far away and I know him only by reminding myself of what I formerly believed and will believe again.

We hold on to the present because we know winter has come. Winter is our time of trial. We have not looked forward to winter, we have not desired or cultivated it, but now it is here, and there is no way around it, no turning back, no slipping around another way. Now it is clear that our faith, poor thing that it is, will be put to the test at last. The people with whom we have always lived, who are part of us, mothers and fathers and grandparents and great-aunts and husbands and lovers and dear ones—they too are on the voyage, and it is also winter for them.

DWINDLING CHOICES, DEEPENING GRACE

One of the most convincing authorities for the reality of spiritual life is Viktor Frankl, who speaks of the power of spirituality for the prisoners in Nazi concentration camps. "In spite of all the enforced physical and mental primitiveness of life in a concentration camp," Frankl writes in *Man's Search for Meaning*, "it was possible for spiritual life to deepen. Sensitive people who were used to a rich intellectual life may have suffered much pain (they were often of a delicate constitution), but the damage to their inner selves was less. They were able to retreat from their terrible surroundings into a life of inner riches and spiritual freedom."[9]

I like the observation made by the theologian Karl Rahner about God. He says God is the answer to the question that I am! In his essay, "Theology and Anthropology," he says that humanity and God are intimately connected, so much so that any statement about one is also about the other. When he says that we know God in and through our most ordinary experience, Rahner makes sense out of the word "grace."[10]

Do we pray differently as we grow older? For some, growing older is the first call to prayer. In one way getting older is in itself an experience of God, a sharper opportunity for grace. We are faced with narrowing options. Intensity is heightened as our choices dwindle. We have to undergo a new experience of conversion, akin to the religious conversions we have already had. I have reason to accept what Thomas Merton says, that we are converted over and over in our lives, and that each such passage is a deeper and more final rending of the self. Now I understand that getting older is another surrender, like the ones before, but having its own special character and its own supply of grace.

G.K. Chesterton says about surrender that it is a moment of narrowness: "That intensity which seems most narrow because it comes to the point, like a medieval window...." In Chesterton's imaginative figure, the person feels "as if he were looking through a leper's window. He is looking through a little crack or crooked hole that seems to grow smaller as he stares at it...."[11]

This surrender that Chesterton describes is not the conscious affirmation of a religious choice. Instead it is what comes before that choice, a moment of abandonment, a sensing of our human boundedness and inadequacy that seems to have extension in space and time. William James describes something similar in different language. He sees surrender of the self as the resolution of a crisis in which the person is "living on the ragged edge of his consciousness, pent in to his sin and want and incompleteness, and consequently unconsolable," and unable to accept an ordinary reassurance that all is well. To him, all is not well. James thinks it is unlikely that such a crisis will be resolved by a "will to believe," the active choosing of a better frame of mind, or by the chance "that an opposite affection should overpoweringly break over us."

James says the solution to such a crisis is an inaction, an undoing: "getting so exhausted with the struggle that we have to stop—so we drop down, give up, and don't care any longer. Our emotional brain-centers strike work, and we lapse into a temporary apathy. Now there is documentary proof that this state of temporary exhaustion not infrequently forms part of the conversion process."[12]

Don't I find myself again in a situation that is closing in, where thought and resolution are useless, but it does help to relent and give in? I can't charge forward to overcome this; instead I have to give way and be led, intuitively, into a space that squeezes me tight. I am like Augustine in the garden, wanting to make a choice but unable to do so, unable to put the will into play. "I was saying inside myself, 'Now, now, let it be now! and as I spoke the words I was already beginning to go in the direction I wanted to go. I nearly managed it, but I did not quite manage it. Yet I did not slip right back to the beginning; I was a stage above that, and I stood there to regain my breath. And I tried again and I was very nearly there; I was almost touching it and grasping it, and then I was not there, I was not touching it...."[13]

Like Augustine, I am hanging in suspense. Like Chesterton, I am in the gap, the abyss "between doing and not doing such a thing...." I am in between the person I was and the person I have not yet become.

SOMETHING MORE IS ASKED OF US

What are all these protestations? Where is all this fear coming from? Relationships with God are confrontational. Demands are being made. An all is being asked, not always dramatically, but firmly. So we do not rush, sometimes, to face this relationship. C.S. Lewis speaks of his relationship to God, his conversion, as being somehow "ambiguous." "As for what we commonly call Will, and what we commonly call Emotion, I fancy these usually talk too loud, protest too much, to be quite believed."[14] Lewis dislikes the formality of religious categories. Instead he insists that in his confrontation what he heard was God saying, "Put down your gun and we'll talk."[15] For Lewis the experience of God is one of dismantling, unbuckling, letting down resistance, ultimately an undoing. "Now I felt... that God was out of reach not because of something I could not do but because of something I could not stop doing. If I could only leave off, let go, unmake myself, I could be there."[16]

There are dozens of similar accounts of surrender. Life presents a series of journeys into the void, scampers through the abyss. Surrender is the necessary undoing for such predicaments, and this surrender does not always bring with it lyrical highs and enthusiastic feelings. Some who have gone through such experiences may give testimonies of joy and appreciation, but their accounts seem non-transferable. Each of us must make our own surrender, in circumstances that seem to be unique. This kind of surrender is unfaith asking for faith, without confidence of deliverance or rescue. The asking is nevertheless a kind of self-giving.

Getting older, then, is giving way to another painful conversion. I like what the theologian Karl Barth says about conversion when he calls it a powerful summons to halt and advance. That, to me, is how it feels: stopped in my tracks by the powerful realization that youth and middle age have been blown away by storms of change. As C.S. Lewis said about his mother's death, "It was sea and islands now; the great continent had sunk like Atlantis."[17]

This alienation is not unbelief. Instead, it takes place within and during a continuing belief that God exists. This aloneness comes because God is not within our power to control; time is not subject to us, but to forces, his forces, beyond our grasp. My alienation is greater than the atheist's; for the God I love and have given my life to will not do it my way; he appears to have forgotten me.

The believer in the suspense of surrender sees God as the rich man did, looking across from hell; knowing there is a blessed vision from which he or she is always to be shut out. The alienation of surrender is knowing that some bliss may exist, but out of our reach; a bliss to which we feel forever not entitled.

Can we look on this insight as a gift? Surrender is the moment when I see clearly (but hopelessly) where I stand before God. This deep intuition of reality is something given, something we ourselves could not bring about.

Like Augustine, Aquinas, Luther, I say: By myself I can do nothing. I surrender, I relent, I undo myself, and grace comes as pure gift.

What about my freedom? Isn't this all paradox? C.S. Lewis says, "I chose, but it did not seem possible to do the opposite."[18] It isn't so much that God's light enters our dark universe at pinpoints: not at all. By a reversal, the truth is a universe filled with light; our *non serviam*, like Lucifer's, keeps us entirely in the dark. The yielding of our surrenders opens us up to a God who is wholly there, a universe already filled with light.

The intervention isn't God's but ours. Our surrender is giving way to death, a helpless descent into baptismal waters, an abandonment to the unknown. This death is entered into for God without a guarantee of God. The view is closing in. Our breathing space is short. Time is running out. This death taken on God's word is what we say conversion is. Our baptism is in the act of self-surrender, not in the waters when they splash.

Now we know how inadequate we are for the gifts of grace poured out on us. In the many surrenders of the spiritual life we remember our first self-gift. Each one is something new, like nothing that went before. The continuing experience of conversion doesn't shout but becomes more quiet and still.

God is in waiting for us. He is accepting the gift we make. He has entered into time for us, to show us that time is more than a cosmic joke. Salvation is an event. God is personal. He has left the ninety-nine to find the one. Justification is not a theory but a story.

MAKING THE GIFT OF SELF

Even as I celebrate what I have learned about praying as a discipline, about the formal side of spiritual life, I remember those who, for one reason or another, possibly in childhood emotional formation, can't experience religion as I do. For them, God is met in other ways, ways that are not mentioned in terms of faith.

Can I ever come to terms with the memory of Oscar's camellias? This was my great-uncle's triumph, the crown of a life well-lived, the growing of a magnificent camellia garden. As I reflect on my memories of Oscar it seems to me that, simply by being closer now to the age he was when I knew him first, I am able to see him more clearly. Is it possible that all my male relatives have been seen through a distorting lens? Did I really know Oscar for the man he was, the dedicated economist and teacher? Now, in a burst of insight, I think I know, that Oscar's camellias were his spirituality, his worship, his celebration of God's creative power.

The camellia is an exquisite plant that does best in sunny climates but also can manage with partial shade. Even without their flowers, camellia bushes are handsome. Their leaves are lustrous, broad, evergreen. But the flowers are the triumph, appearing, as they do in winter as a unexpected blessing, a kind of stunt performed by nature at a time when we least expect it. There are single, semi-double, and double forms of camellias, ranging up to as much as four inches across: whites, pinks, red, and variegated colors.

When Oscar retired he began to grow camellias. Perhaps he had been growing them all along, but I only began to know about it when I was in college (this would be 1953 through 1957) when boxes of Oscar's camellias came by post. I remember them now in all their fragility and power: the boxes opened to reveal layers of frail, passionate camellias packed in wet paper, packed with attentiveness and care. They had names; each one was a triumph. We floated them in shallow crystal bowls on side tables, on coffee tables, in the entranceway, in the dining room of the house on Arabella Street where the high ceilings and handsome wallpaper, the mahogany staircase, and the glass chandeliers sparkled in a kind of retelling of past revels and future celebrations.

It was winter! It is in winter that Louisiana camellias bloom. This, too, was part of Oscar's triumph, getting his garden to bloom earlier in winter than if nature had taken her course. The gardener must protect his plants from low spots in which cold air settles, from destructive winds, from late, damaging frosts. The scientist as well as the nature-lover must bring his skill to bear, planting the camellias where they have the best sheltering by natural or man-made walls, shrubbery, and garden fences. To do this properly, the gardener has to understand how wind reacts when it meets a barrier.

If the barrier is a solid fence or wall, the wind jumps up over it like a hurdle, comes down on the other side, and keeps going. The only plants protected by the wall are those in the immediate lee. In Louisiana, plants are often covered during frosts; sometimes, if they are planted in tubs, they can be moved indoors. Whatever it takes, it takes skill and attention, energy and commitment, and most of all, love.

In my memory now I reconstruct Oscar's loving gift of growing camellias for us. No doubt they were also for himself, his personal celebration of existence. This was the self-gift of his old age, to devote his intellect, his planning, his management talent, his fully lived economics, to the beauty of a winter garden, a hymn to the beauty of God.

CELEBRATING TODAY

It is morning. Again, we-who-are-becoming-old are drinking our coffee, taking our vitamins, snuggling into our dressing gowns. What or who is to prevent us from remaining in this instant forever, with the morning papers stretched out before us? What is this relentless power that draws us, minute by minute, into the future, leaving no time for hesitation or doubt? How can we dance to the music that pulls us forward?

"I could leave the world with today in my eyes," Sook tells Buddy in Capote's story, trying to explain how wrong she was about the presence of God in our lives. Sook had always thought she would have to be sick and dying before she saw the Lord. Now she knows better. She once thought that when he came it would be like "looking at a Baptist window: pretty as colored glass with the sun pouring through." Now she guesses that the Lord has already shown himself, breaking through in our everyday lives. She speculates that things as they are, including grass and sky and a dog pawing earth for a bone in the Alabama countryside—just what she has always known was knowing him. It is a message Capote writes down for all of us, a message he remembers all his life.

Fruitcake weather! These words from Capote's story come back like a refrain, signalling the pull of time. Through the chill days, as our lives experience a turning into winter, we will keep on moving into the future, and it is now that our love of God, if it can be said to be love after all, will come to its moment of darkness and confrontation.

CHAPTER THREE

Prayer as Navigation

IN GERSHWIN'S TOUCHING OPERA Porgy tells Bess that the sorrow of the past is all undone. The real happiness, he tells her, has just begun. The same note of renewal and new beginnings is struck in the Song of Songs: "For see, the winter is past, the rains are over and gone, the flowers appear on the earth. The season of glad songs has come, the cooing of the turtledove is heard in our land."[1]

Is it possible now that there is a renewal, a freshness, not only in my heart, but in the hearts of many others? Is it because of who we are, or possibly how long we have lived, how much we have grasped the nettle of what it is to be alive? Renewal is freshness, new life springing up, old ways and wounds forgotten and healed. Such is the current awakening in many American hearts: the renewed American experience of prayer. No doubt a strong, fresh spirituality is broadly at work.

Speaking about this phenomenon in *The New York Times Maga-*

zine in the 1980s, Kenneth Briggs wrote: "The current yearning for deeply personal, in-depth prayer signifies that the spiritual revival of the mid-1970s... has taken some new directions. The earlier phase was marked by outward revivalism and dramatic conversion, the newer phase emphasizes the inward nurture of the soul and a deepening of faith." Briggs was especially documenting "a new breed of spiritual directors" and contrasting their approach with crisis-oriented, hot-line, problem-and-solution prayer.[2] However, the prayer phenomenon now going on is too varied, too diverse, too rich to be neatly categorized. Spiritual direction is only one phase of the changing tides of prayer. What seems to be happening is a massive shift from the structured devotions of the past with specific tasks to be fulfilled, to ongoing personal relationships with God, neighbor, and community, nurtured by prayer, group sharing, retreats, liturgy, and community service. It is becoming commonplace to hear everyday people speak of their prayer lives or their own personal "spirituality." Many Christians are coming to understand and live the idea of community in a way that goes far beyond what happens in church. Expectations are rising. Spiritual friendship, support groups, and structured relationships with qualified spiritual directors and mentors are part of it all.

In fact, while the sense of newness and renewal is strong, experience suggests that what is happening is more old than new: a contemporary recapturing of ancient vitality in Christian prayer. The Western church has its own history of mysticism and mountaintop experience, usually confined to the monastery or the cloister. The sixteenth century broke spirituality open for lay participation. Now what is happening is a further development, in which all the faithful feel called, deeply and radically, to intimacy with God. Even the word "vocation" is now being restored to its ancient meaning as the universal Christian call to holiness.

A PRAYER RENAISSANCE

It seems that America's faithful are on a collective journey. The ancient prayer traditions of Christian faith are now being recovered as resources for our contemporary lives. We are trying to get in touch with our roots and to live the ancient spirit of prayer every day. If Francis de Sales is looking on; he should be pleased, for he is one who centuries ago was already insisting that prayer could be practiced as a regimen by people in every walk of life.

Along with this prayer revival comes a renaissance in the publishing and republishing of spiritual works. Many familiar spiritual classics are being retranslated and modernized. Systems of spirituality from the past are being interpreted through a new lens, to make a long-honored tradition practical for modern believers.

Among my favorites are such mystical writers as Teresa of Avila, John of the Cross, Thérèse of Lisieux, all in the Carmelite tradition; Lady Julian of Norwich and the unknown author of *The Cloud of Unknowing;* among seventeenth-century resources one could do no better than DeCaussade's *Abandonment to Divine Providence;* and there are modern prayer instructors in profusion. Helpful books include those by William Johnston, especially *Silent Music* and *The Inner Eye of Love;* just about everything by Henri Nouwen and Richard Foster; Thomas Green, *Opening to God* and *Darkness in the Marketplace;* Basil Pennington's *Daily We Touch Him* and *Centering Prayer.* For meditation and reflection the poetic passages of Scripture are very useful and evocative, including the prophets and the psalms.

Another source with the same depth is mystical poetry from all the centuries. My own favorites along these lines are George Herbert and John Donne, and other Christian poets of the seventeenth century, as well as nineteenth-century Christian visionaries including Emily Dickinson and Gerard Manley Hopkins. The literature on prayer from Christian sources is vast, but dipping into any established modern or classical work can provide a banquet of insights and refreshment.

THE BAPTIZED IMAGINATION

One of the greatest resources in the present renewal is not literature so much as imagination itself. In his own story of conversion, C.S. Lewis describes the baptizing of his imagination as one stage in his spiritual journey. While reading a novel by George MacDonald in a railway carriage, Lewis found a way to experience the possibility of holiness. "That night," he says, "my imagination was, in a certain sense, baptized. The rest of me, not unnaturally, took longer."[3]

Reason, for earlier generations, was a critical tool, a cornerstone in the edifice of belief. Today, that is still true for some. But as doctrine is less emphatic, intuition and imagination have taken the stronger role.

How clear it is that before one can believe in God, one must imagine the sort of God it is possible to know! Speaking of the Nazi persecutions, a friend of mine explained that she could not believe in God because (in holding God responsible for these hideous events) she would be bound to hate him. Her preferred solution to the dilemma was to will God out of existence! In such cases what is needed is a deep relenting, a forgiving process in which we allow ourselves to imagine a God who loves us, has the universe well in hand, entertaining the possibility that he who hung the stars and made the planets loved us into existence as well. (In contrast with my friend's denial of God, Elie Wiesel tells a story of prayer in the Nazi concentration camps. A trial was held by Jewish inmates in one of these camps; God was found guilty of all charges against him; after which the community adjourned to pray.)

In our prayer lives, then, we are re-imagining a God with

whom conversation is possible. This reverent imagining helps us to shatter false images: a God who exists but forgot about us; a God who existed for unlettered folk but not for intellectuals; a God who might exist for philosophy or mathematics but couldn't be reached by phone; a hard taskmaster, unforgiving judge, life force, and so on. Out of our own memories we retrieve (so as to deal with them) angers and grievances. From those relived experiences of God we begin to picture him in sharper focus. Now we can permit God to approach us, we can accept an intimate friendship with him. For some what is needed is not approachability but transcendence. Imagination frees us to find the end of our searching, the Lord our hearts are yearning for. Through imaginative freedom we may glimpse God as a blazing sun of justice, a Yahweh who stoops down to lift up the infant, a generous Creator who knows how to give good things to his children, or the protective Lord we knew in our childhood lullaby.

"It was as though the voice which had called to me from the world's end were now speaking by my side," C.S. Lewis explains.

"It was with me in the room, or in my own body, or behind me.... It seemed to have been always with me....."[4]

BEGINNING: FIRST AND LAST

My own sense of prayer is that the most critical moment is beginning, but prayer has no necessary sequence.[5]

Instead, in my view, prayer is a jewel with many facets. Beginning is not only first but last and in-between as well. As John Henry Newman says, "we are *ever* but beginning."[6] The point is to capture prayer almost as Audubon might have, in its wilderness setting, on the wing. The seven facets as I see them are: beginning; yielding; darkness; transparency; fear of heights (fear of advancing in the spiritual life); hoops of steel (spiritual friendship, fellowship, and community); and clinging, an expression—both biblical and theological—for what used to be called (by some is still called) unitive prayer.

How is it, everyone wants to know, that experiences of such depth can happen in our midst, even in middle-class humdrum lives? The answer is biblical, that God is no respecter of persons, not class conscious, and shows no partiality. He distributes his riches even to members of the middle class, once they have laid down their hostile defenses and surrendered to his will.

LETTING DOWN DEFENSES

Does the Lord actually speak to us in a language we can recognize? Does he speak as he used to in the desert with Moses and our ancestors? We learn how God communicates only after we take some chances. When we squash the reluctances that say, "I don't have time to pray," "God talks to other people, not to me," "I don't know what you're talking about. Nothing happens when I pray," or even, "I'm so busy serving the Lord, I don't have time to pray," when we set all these unconvincing excuses aside—when we yield, when we surrender—that is when actual dialogue can begin.

When we start to drop defenses, we learn (or relearn) that breakdowns in prayer stem less from lack of time, hardly from God's indifference, more likely from some common ailment of ours like fear. Once we know prayer is real, that God is accessible, what often holds us back is reluctance to get involved. We worry that something might be required. Dues will certainly have to be paid. How Christian of us, really! We're afflicted with Peter's fear—we can almost hear ourselves saying, "I never knew the man."

But once we make a surrender of the imagination, other surrenders also may come more easily. Here in the country of the heart, where the Lord can call us by name, we have a sense that almost anything can happen. The table is spread in the wilderness, and we are invited to a picnic after all. We know we are sinners yet we know we are loved. The generous spirit of the Lord is anointing us with forgiveness and acceptance. These are the delights of giving way, with all our faults and feelings, to prayer.

This is no mysticism of the mountaintop. Instead, we are living out our day-to-day existence, traveling back and forth to jobs, to daily errands and chores. There are needy parents asking for more of us, relatives who want more visits, ask for more of our time. In church and parish we may make generous time commitments, then hold back with those who are closest. How can we give ourselves to prayer with this lot setting up their daily whine? Small trials and annoyances crisscross our days. In this wilderness there is prophetic truth. If we would deny ourselves it is best to do it in the wilderness of every day.

WALKING BY FAITH

Two of the most important aspects of the spiritual life are darkness and transparency. Darkness is an actual experience of confusion and abandonment, of walking by faith without seeing the way. For those who have been raised to think Christian belief is a matter of having all the answers, having a neat-and-tidy world view with no cobwebs in the corners, the plain fact of darkness may seem something like betrayal, a disappointment or letdown at the very least.

But the truth of prayer is, the more we trust in God, the more he calls us into the mystery of things and wants us to share his own experience of the cross. The surprise is, he lets us do this wherever and whoever we are, as long as we are willing to pray. Such praying does not even have to be fully attentive, disciplined contemplation. One can spend time with God even when not entirely praying—linger on the edge of his consciousness, enjoy him as a companion or presence just over there, somewhere. God isn't always dazzling. Sometimes he is merely friendly. In any event it is our assent that lets him respond to our need.

Alongside this darkness there is transparency: a kind of seeing through the veil, grasping experience more deeply in and through the Lord, because of the Lord. Transparency is a way of describing the effects of prayer without offering guarantees, without referring to specific gifts and blessings like those promised in Isaiah 11 and Galatians 5. Instead of viewing the transforming effects of prayer as attributes of the holy person, it's possible to look out at the world from the viewpoint of the one who prays, and find the world more open, more available than before. The person of prayer finds God intensely in "things" and yet is less attached to things. The immediacy of experience makes one speak, as the school of Duns Scotus did, in terms of *thisness*, the vision of God in the particular.

By a large shift in our understanding we are plunged into the heart and mystery of things as they are. Who knows where the vision will lead? The call is to come where loving our neighbor might happen without much effort, where forgiveness is not through clenched teeth, but more easygoing. Slowly that stubborn lump of anger or resentment inside of us starts to melt, we sense that we are being healed, we take up our beds and walk.

FRIENDSHIP AS SOUL-GRAPPLING

Perhaps the most striking gift of the spirit in our everyday praying is something I call—borrowing Shakespeare's language—hoops of steel. "Those friends thou hast, and their adoption tried/Grapple them unto thy soul with hoops of steel."[7] This well-documented union of souls is biblical, glimpsed in the love of David and Jonathan, found in the tenderness of Paul and Timothy, mirrored in the intimacy of Augustine and Monica, the passion of Paula and Jerome, the sweet austerity of Benedict and Scholastica.

Holiness, it seems, can fuse hearts. "No man is an island unto himself. Every man is a piece of the continent...."[8]

In contemporary life, spiritual direction is just one chance for close spiritual friendship. In prayer groups, such spiritual partnerships come about easily. Spiritual friendship is something that can't be orchestrated or arranged. But it seems to spring up like dandelions wherever people are gathered in Christ's name.

Spirituality is lifelong. And it is usually surprising. Prayer is not always a source of consolation, more often a matter of holding the line, having to keep at it without warm feelings, when memories hurt, things don't go well, resentments escalate. If we look ahead the way can be forbidding. Yet if we look behind, the complex path shows us how far we have come. We notice how the road twists. We see that we have chosen the Lord again and again, whatever the discipline required, and we see in retrospect that he has not failed us.

There may be things we wanted, things we did not get, rewards that did not come. We must wrestle with haunting memories, disappointments, disenchantments, competitions where we were losers and others won. Even so we cling to the Lord. We know he cares for us. By faith we hold on.

Gradually, we begin to understand that our prayer has passed far beyond technique, beyond the longing for personal growth, past customary notions of fulfillment. Instead we are clinging less and less to motivational language, and fastening more and more onto the Lord. Prayer is less a matter of petitions, rarely a matter of encounters. We have ceased to wonder whether that figure who met us on the hillside might possibly have been the Lord. Instead there is an intimacy that passes our understanding. We are held in a clasp that is loving and powerful, one that makes demands. Yet we know we have chosen this, our commitment is rooted, radical. There is no slipping loose, no turning back. The path lies straight ahead.

But generalizing about the interior content of prayer is possibly misleading or may raise false expectations. God's way with each one is precisely what is right for each, and nobody ought to wish for someone else's experience. It is tempting, but dangerous, to compare and contrast. Also, to be preoccupied with the glittering extras, voices, and visions and such stuff, is something about which spiritual advisors will likely caution us. The so-called fruits of prayer: peacefulness, forbearance, temperance, fortitude, and so forth, should also be treated with care. There's a danger in wanting to become accomplished in prayer, a danger in the instinct to show off one's prayer experiences for public admiration. Always, we need to be reminded to cling to the Lord and not to the experience—consolation or desolation—of prayer.

GROUPS MAY STRENGTHEN US

In another way, groups are healthy. Highly romantic prayer experiences often have their funny moments. In group sharing the lighter side of life tends to surface. Burdens become more bearable when shared among members of a group. Community is strengthening. We understand our experiences are authentic. At the same time we see that the point of prayer is to make us more loving and generous. This happens, not all at once, but in good time and, unselfconsciously, as we pray and share our experience in an easy, natural way.

Openness to the needs of others is an almost inevitable consequence. Also, we develop some real detachment about the things we use and own. Most importantly, we come to want deeper conversion, the next step in the adventure. Together and separately, we are ready for the Lord's call.

A good description of the maturing and stabilizing influence of prayer can be found in the promises of Alcoholics Anonymous. This program of everyday spirituality is based on a practical surrender to the limits imposed by a perilous addiction. It requires complete reliance on God by people who in many instances have not been able to handle the demands and rites of established religion. Clearly, the Alcoholics Anonymous promises celebrate the blessings of Christian prayer.

In part they say: "We are going to know a new freedom and a new happiness. We will not regret the past nor wish to shut the door on it. We will comprehend the word 'serenity' and we will know peace. No matter how far down the scale we have gone, we will see how our experiences can benefit others. That feeling of uselessness and self-pity will disappear. We will lose interest in selfish things and gain interest in our fellows. Self-seeking will slip away. Our whole attitude and outlook on life will change. Fear of people and economic insecurity will leave us. We will intuitively know how to handle situations which used to baffle us. We will suddenly realize that God is doing for us what we could not do for ourselves."[9] Developed in a practical and spiritual program to maintain sobriety, these promises are the fruit of lived experience. AA members experience conversion and live their faith courageously in the context of each day.

We are called both to Christian maturity and to childhood simplicity. All this potentially is ours when we become teachers and examples for one another; when we extend to each other the experience of friendship, commitment, and hope.

The journey is ongoing. We yield, naming our experience pilgrimage, growth, maturation, a personal and collective voyage of faith. While both conversion and prayer can be captured in structures and discerned in terms of stages and steps, they are, like all love relationships, spontaneous, unpredictable, blown by winds of grace.

NOT WHAT WE DO, WHAT GOD DOES

No doubt our activist mentality as Americans and Westerners is what causes us to focus repeatedly on the style, the manner, the mechanics, the method of prayer. How should we schedule our devotions? Must we pray in common or alone? Is there a risk that solitary prayer will make hermits out of us? Is it better to pray with or without mental images, with or without words? Should we beseech the Lord or just remain in God's presence? How much time, realistically, should ordinary persons spend in prayer? All these questions are practical, legitimate, worthy of attention, able on the whole to be answered by those who are experienced. Yet to focus on these things, too much, too often, may be a distraction from the main point of praying. Our focus should not be on what we do but what the Lord does in us.

In contrast, an activist mentality of another sort measures prayer in terms of its social effects, links prayer to justice and political action. This prayer-activism is desirable, legitimate, so long as it doesn't take on a mentality of works-righteousness. "By their fruits you shall know them" is now, as always, a proper measure for the depth of spiritual life.

Ultimately, however, the meaning of spirituality is beyond specific tasks and actions, missions, and agendas. The transforming effects pass beyond description, too. Even such metaphors as Jesus used—the dragnet, the man who found a buried treasure, and the like—seem to falter or fall short. Words, phrases, images, everything fails to describe fully what our relationship with God is about.

Because we want to pray well, proficiently, we concentrate on the practical and specific. From everywhere we pluck the wealth of good advice on how to pray effectively: "Take a few moments to settle quietly... be aware of your body... try to focus your mind in your heart, and then gather there your energies... humbly acknowledge that you are in the presence of God... try to be totally open... rest in God's presence, listening..." Such suggestions are simple, spare, useful. They will do the job of instructing and recalling us to the simple ways of prayer.

Beyond our private prayer times, the collective prayer of worshipping Christians provides us with an overarching tent to house us, gathering us together from East and West, North and South.

But the more important change is beyond structures, beyond words and images. It is a kingdom of hope that comes to exist in our minds and hearts, a sense of expectation. We are called, we are summoned, we are going somewhere, we are on the road, and the Lord is both at the destination and walking the path with us.

To live the experience of prayer is to enter into a mystery with the Lord. It is the mystery we share every time we celebrate the Eucharist together, in the collective partaking of his blood and body, but not only then. It is also a mystery lived out in less conspicuous ways, when we extend ourselves, when we stretch beyond limits, when we pour ourselves out for the kingdom's sake. It is the mystery we share when we are pierced by the violence and evil of the world, when our hearts are broken by treachery and war. It is the mystery we share when we are passionate for the Lord's coming. It is the mystery we share when we ask how to carry more of the cross. It is the mystery we share when we dream, or envision the possibility of peace not only someday but in our own times and our own generation.

It is the mystery we share when we become childlike and are willing to trust at least a little that things make sense. It is the mystery we share when we visit the sick, welcome the stranger, when we extend ourselves for others.

In the growing experience of Christian prayer—private and public, collective and solitary—a good spirit is at work. It is a spirit of repentance. We have understood freshly that we are not coming to church to be ministered to, but to minister, not to be served, but to serve. In our yielding and our surrender we have taken hold of our own salvation, ready to work it out in fear and trembling. The guilt of the past is gone. We do not punish ourselves with what we have not done, for we are learning that anxiety is the devil's tool, and part of our cross of hyperachievement. Instead, we learn how to be with the Lord in simple ways. Obediently, we render up our work, our skills, our talents, to him and to others for his sake. The spirit of our renewal, then, is a spirit of encouragement and hope.

CHAPTER FOUR

Night Fears

MY MOTHER HAS HAD A FALL. This time she has fallen at the breakfast table, from her customary chair where she sits every morning to read the paper. In reaching for the second section of the *Times-Picayune*, only a few inches beyond her fingertips, she has slipped entirely from the silky upholstered dining room chair. Now she lies flat on the floor, looking upward at the ceiling and laughing. Her cane is stretched out beside her. I am also laughing, but inwardly I am afraid. It takes us a few moments to get her up, to reestablish her dignity in the spot she generally occupies. From that location she can resume giving orders: "I need the sugar. Please bring me a spoon. I need the ice in this glass to be chipped smaller than this, and please bring me a second glass with just water, very little ice, filled to the top. Also I need my vitamin." No sound of the word please anywhere. After a short silence, there is an embarrassed thank you.

Immediately, as if to refute this distress, a second scene flashes to mind: an image of my mother completely in command. I see her in a fashionable taupe wool coat, smart gold earrings, black kid gloves crushed at the wrist, a handsome dark wool dress, imported calf-skin shoes and handbag. She is the ideal CEO, completely in charge, Helen to many, Mrs. Dietrich to everyone. Even to me she is often Mrs. Dietrich in my imagination. I know her as the person who founds companies, launches ventures, develops the potential of employees, hatches creative business proposals and ideas. Now that she is aging, slipping, she is still Mrs. Dietrich to the bank executives, lawyers, and CPAs with whom I must deal in her behalf. Never, I think, can I fill her shoes. Even on the checkbook she is Mrs. Helen Dietrich while I am simply Emilie Griffin. No one can displace this towering figure in my imagination. Though she is merely five feet two, she is larger than life; she reigns.

"I think in your mother's next career she should become Queen of England," says David Bendix, her former court reporting associate, as we sketch out plans for a party in her honor to be held at the New Orleans Board of Trade. David is partly spoofing about Helen's membership in a number of hereditary societies; but mostly he's acknowledging her capacity to wield the scepter, on most occasions, with high humor and a kind of glee. Helen has style. The Dietrich dazzle is unmistakable, I reflect once again, knowing that for me the name and the business enterprise she founded in the tourism field will always be one and the same.

I am the one in denial; Helen is dealing with her old age better than I; I myself am fighting against not only her old age but my own.

It becomes clear to me, as perhaps it has not done until now, that everything will have to change. This apartment will have to be sold in order to satisfy the mortgage and pay debts. My mother will need to move in with us, but that requires some engineering, possibly some adaptation of our rooms. Will we need a special chair fitting for the staircase? Is other work needed? My mother will not be restored to independent living again. And my husband and I will not be able to pay the mortgages on her home and our own, while affording help for her at the same time.

MID-LIFE FANTASIES

Less than an hour later as I rummage through the library books to be returned, I find this passage in Doris Lessing's novel, *The Summer Before the Dark:*

> Kate sat under the tree in such a way that her body was in the shade, and her legs were stretched into the sun as if they were stockingless. She was examining her large square house in its large garden. She did this like someone saying goodbye, but that was only because she and her husband had recently been saying that now the children would soon be altogether grown it, it might be time to start thinking of getting themselves something smaller? A flat? They could buy a house in the country and share it with friends—perhaps the Finchleys.
>
> Kate often thought about this, but as of something that was years off.[1]

In Lessing's novel Kate is an Englishwoman at mid-life who goes to work as a language interpreter for an organization called Global Food. Her assignment takes her to a conference in Turkey. There she decides to have an affair with a man much younger than herself, and they travel together through Europe. Meantime Kate's husband is on business overseas, as he often is.

It is the perfect mid-life fantasy acted out. In some part of us we think the sexual encounter is the height of our experience. As our youth ebbs we look to recapture it by having random love matches or fantasizing about casual affairs. Like Captain Queeg with his strawberries, we look to repeat some past success, to relive some earlier triumph. Fiction and romance novels reinforce this impulse, give us chances to repeat the daydream. In reading them we relive the sexual encounter with its high drama and sense of wonder. What on earth can compare with the exquisiteness of the chase, seeking and being sought after? Hearing the other person say sweet things provides some slender reassurance of who we are.

But does it? Doesn't the aging woman with the younger male companion know what falsehoods she is clinging to? Can't she guess the things being said about her behind her back? What about that older gent, glimpsed in the elevator the morning after with that female young enough to be his daughter? Does he really believe his security lies in being sexually powerful? Then, what must he think when that security begins to ebb, when he feels he's not the man he was?

It's easy to laugh at the stereotypes, much harder to see the truth in ourselves; a strange twist of vision moves us in the wrong direction, drives us to sin; sin is hurtful self-wrong, something seized as a good which is in fact not a good but an evil. We are like the storks, migrating from the north of Europe into the Sinai desert, whose bodies are too exhausted to make the full journey. Some inner, migratory survival instinct sends us into an unknown which is unhealthy for us; but it is our own good we are seeking.

SEX AS FRIEND AND ENEMY

But is the sex drive really our enemy? Can't it befriend us when we handle it in the service of God? The predicament of Sarah Ferguson springs to mind. Ferguson is a beautiful woman, the ripples of her long red hair stun the eye. She is young. She seems ripe in every sense of the word. Bulbs flash, cameras roll: there she poses for well-wishers in her engagement scene, in a handsome navy blue suit on the Balmoral lawn; there she poses in her elaborate wedding gown; later she appears with children in her arms, the image of maternal beauty, a madonna worth admiring.

The next pictures are not nearly so winsome. There is Sarah naked from the waist up, her uncovered breasts looking sad as the tabloid paparrazi expose her to the world's judgment and ridicule. In a world where reputation is everything, Sarah is destroyed.

Sarah becomes the stork driven south into the Sinai desert. Instinct has carried her in a false direction. Now she must live in exile from the blinding stardust of her former life.

How are we to keep a proper footing in each stage of the life journey? Only by grace will we come through; otherwise we too will stumble and fall. To be more truthful, we ourselves have already fallen, yet our falls from grace are not so public as Sarah's; we have managed to hide our little escapades or we have driven our sexuality inward, hiding it underneath fat-folds of repression and denial. No one is exempt from the power-drive that leads into sin and self-will. Wherever, whoever we are, we may lose our way. Longing for mastery and power, we want to hold back time. When we are young, we rush to sample the full range of human emotions, afraid of missing something, of having our lives pass without meaning, without event. What, we think, if we became old and knew we had missed it all? Yet in the randomness of casual friendships and affairs, in uncommitted relationships, we find no permanence, nothing to hold on to. Commitment is the only way; if we want satisfaction and safety we can't find it by a scramble over the wall.

Now youth is behind us; we have shouldered the heavy commitments of maturity; we have come through, carried the load—mortgages, loans, entanglements, debt. At last we see in ourselves and others the signs of old age. How are we now to behave? Are we supposed to spend the rest of our lives doing small tasks, falling asleep in front of blinking television screens with newspapers over our faces? What, if anything, lies ahead? Have we missed everything, after all?

At mid-life we discovered and developed our spiritual lives; possibly we embraced them so fully that this spirituality of ours became a new form of relentless pursuit; far from a letting go or a surrender, the learning of a new vocabulary and a new way of living and believing took center stage; we gave our lives over to a new spiritual enterprise.

Possibly also we refurbished our dreams. Coming through tough times, we have found our deepest springs of creativity; we returned to the fundamentals of our life-ambitions; we remembered and tried to affirm again what we once believed in. This brought a freshness, a renewal. We felt young all over again. Falling in love with God was ecstatic, delirious, intoxicating. This new and passionate discovery took years off our lives.

But as with our first fervor, this second or third fervor of mid-life begins to ebb; now in fact we are faced with a life-passage that can never be confused with youth. This is the hard slog into a future that does not seem unlimited. In front of us there is a wall, and the wall does not seem to be a wall that we can scale.

A new kind of discouragement plagues me with questions.

In my forties and fifties, haven't I lived my life already? Haven't I plunged deeply into experience, amassing achievements, building friendships, reinforcing family ties, doing community service, receiving awards? Does anything remain to be done? Is it time now to retreat from the fray, to stop trying, to go out in the woods somewhere and find a Walden to rest in? Do I understand or embrace the possibility of rest? Do I regard play and leisure as false paths, inauthentic and empty because they serve no one but myself?

Now my future has caught up with me. My mother requires full-time attention. She must be helped from the bedroom to the bath, to the breakfast table and back again to the big chair. Someone must lovingly bring her the newspaper, the television log, the glass of ice chipped just so, the telephone, the mail. The Lord has engaged me in this service. I am called, I am here to serve, I am a part of the scheme. But why don't I feel the grace of it, the consolation?

Tied now forever—no, not forever, but for the rest of my mother's life, which I want to be forever—to this way of living, I am captured, caught in time. But wasn't I always caught in time?

I remember in a rush how it once felt to have young children, to be awakened each morning by a squall. I remember the long hours watching Sesame Street, Mister Rogers, the Electric Company, Captain Kangaroo. When was I ever free? Before I had children, I wanted them, I was assailed by fears that they would never come to exist. Before I had a husband, I dreamed of him, of how he would be, of the life we would build together. I chased him in fear that he might not exist! Always I have been in a dance of commitments not yet made but dreamed of, rebelling against alliances and entanglements already made. Sarah Ferguson and I and the Colonel's Lady and Rosie O'Grady are sisters under the skin!

DELUSIONS OF FREEDOM

The sexual encounter is a moment of apparent freedom, but the freedom is delusionary. Beyond the walls are the photojournalists, moralists who will make us answer to the whole judgmental world. These people of the world who judge us, they will not tolerate our transgressions, our adulterous love-play beside swimming pools in the South of France! Not while others have to pay income tax, stand in lines at the post office, pay motor vehicle fines, take tests for the driver's license. How the moralists and pharisees reprove the duchess, finding her unworthy of her royal state! More serious than these caviling critics is the inner moralist, the voice within that calls us to a goodness we feel we can't achieve. This is our governing belief system, the one that calls us to live an ideal. We have never been free of these inner voices, these powerful demands.

Even so, I want to be footloose. I want to be that cowboy on the plain who has nothing to answer to except the dogies and the overarching sky: don't fence me in! Yet fast and loose is not footloose. In the fast lane there is a kind of anguish far beyond mine; among those who burn the candle at both ends is a fear that will never be set to rest. My fear is as nothing to that fear. Or possibly, all fear is a kind of death.

"Whoever keeps my word will never see death."[2] We live not only in a physical space but we also swim in inner consciousness. The only possible human freedom lies in a comfort zone within that consciousness. Freedom comes as a realization that one is loved, accepted, in the deepest sense, secure. Men and women in later life who run scared from a lack of acceptance, trying to find relationships that make them comfortable and set them free, fail to recognize that only one fundamental relationship is ever fully dependable and secure. "With God on our side, who can be against us?"[3] The Lord is near to those who call, supportive to those who know his name. Intimate friendship with God sets us free.

Saddled with painful life circumstances, it is easy to blame God for our woes. The answer to this vicious circle of thought? A breakthrough must be made in the spirit, through the spiritual imagination. We have to remember and believe that God's wisdom is greater than our own.

Prayer and worship are ways of grasping what is real and true. By facing the boundaries of our existence we move beyond them; by confronting our sulkiness and anger we stifle their inner tyranny. Acceptance, intimacy with God, lets us break through barriers of space and time. Knowing God as friend and lover is a move for freedom. It is not so much an escape as a surrender, a yielding to God's mastery of our lives; we find ourselves set free not by doing but undoing, by relenting and forgiving, becoming heirs to hope.

FAME'S LAST INFIRMITY

One of the false paths is fame. We suppose that by building monuments to ourselves we will elude the tock of time. This commonplace way of thinking is entirely delusionary. Empire-building, whether through dynastic families or in office towers, is often the material of tragedy.

Arranged in cartoon patterns on the cover of a Sunday magazine, the faces of Elvis Presley and Richard Nixon remind us of the hollowness of empires. Massive libraries in California, massive plantations in Tennessee, will not confer the necessary grace of salvation. It is through God alone that we pass through prison walls and are delivered from the crippling bondage of time.

"Do not reject me now I am old, nor desert me now my strength is failing.... I promise that, ever hopeful, I will praise you more and more.... Now that I am old and gray, God, do not desert me...."[4]

What about immortality? Mostly it is a confusing idea, in conflict with our experience of time, confounding the imagination. Recently I was asked if I wanted to do a certain project for the sake of my posterity. All at once I remembered my daughter Sarah saying, "You think too much, Ma, about your posterity."

Each one of us wants identity. Each one wants to make a contribution. In *The House of the Seven Gables* by Nathaniel Hawthorne, a woman is told that she will begin to experience truth now that she has begun to work for something. But to work for immortality, for a legacy, for the sake of posterity? These are false paths and fools' errands, indeed.

It is glorious and at the same time chilling to watch a film performance by one of the great dance teams: Ginger Rogers and Fred Astaire. There they twirl on a Manhattan roof, captured on film like china figures dancing together on a music box. Caught in their celluloid immortality, the great movie stars of the past repeat their performances word for word, flawlessly, gesture by gesture, at a flip of the VCR. If we aspire to a kind of immortality, surely it must be more than this, to repeat a moment of near perfection over and over. Life is a matter of surprises: but the butterfly in lucite is beyond surprise, immobilized, not immortalized.

THOSE IMMORTAL VISIONS

What sort of immortality do we hope for? Perhaps immortality is the wrong word after all, a leftover from Greek and Roman religions that no one has practiced for centuries. The Norse and the Celts have their own immortal visions: the island of the Arthurian legend swims in the sea off the north coast somewhere, a Bali Hai that may call us any night, any day. Each of us is summoned by our own special home, a dream that blooms in the hillside and shines in the stream.

Resurrection as promised to us is inconceivable. What could it possibly be? Then we shall know even as we are known. We can aspire, at least, to a passionate and dynamic kind of knowing, a resurrected knowing, a beatific knowing, completely flooded and drenched by the love of God. This is a moment we can only guess at from moments of transcendence in the here and now, from human love, from reunions of the heart, from moments of insight, from breakthroughs in forgiveness, from embraces and reconciliations, from moments of high ecstasy in prayer.

Our ancestors took the biblical images at face value, supposing they would be given a pair of golden slippers at heaven's door. Our contemporary jokes about St. Peter at the pearly gates reveal how hard it is to believe that God will keep his promise. "There were three men who met St. Peter at the pearly gates, an Irishman, a Vietnamese, and a hippie, and St. Peter said...."

Yet the yearning for heaven is very deep. This longing for heaven was never so plain as in a book by Geoff Ryman called *Was*.[5] Knowing my interest in the Oz-metaphor, my son has given me the book for my fifty-seventh birthday. Only the slightest glance convinces me that it is a lyrical book about memory and pain. To compound the experience, I choose to read it while waiting in a long line on a hot summer's day at the Department of Public Safety and Corrections of the State of Louisiana. I must wait four and a half hours in line before the officer reviews my proof of insurance and charges me a fine. In this little purgatory I am swept away by Ryman's imaginative interweaving of Los Angeles, California, and Kansas, the intersections of the lives of Judy Garland, Frank Baum, the mystical Dorothy Gale, the historical Dorothy Gael, and a man named Jonathan who is dying of AIDS. Ryman persuades me again of what I already know: all country is heart country. John Milton's insight is fundamental: "The mind is its own place, and in itself/can make a heaven of hell, a hell of heaven."[6]

What does it signify to live long? Ryman's long-suffering hero, Jonathan, is thirty-eight and knows he will not live to see the year 2000. To me, as a believer, his emptiness, (as with many of the book's characters) seems like a failure to know that he is deeply loved by God. This is the hollowness of the book. Its chilling ironies are jokes against God. Aunty Em's religious zeal is a mockery; Uncle Henry's sexual history is heartbreak; across the American landscape there is no sign of Glinda the Good Witch of the North. These are T.S. Eliot's hollow men and women, their heads and bodies are stuffed with straw. The Kansas wind whistles through them.

Look, look, he's right over there! I remember how in my first days of religious conversion I saw God on stage as the silent player in the theater of the absurd. While Lucky and Pozzo and Estragon and Vladimir waited for the Godot who never came, I saw God's presence in and through them, and wanted, like the child at her first theatrical, to shout from the audience, "Look! You're missing the whole thing! He's right over there!"

But where is this over there, when the Lord is everywhere? Our unwillingness, our obstinacy, our determination to do it all on our own, without help from Anyone, this is the deep source of our anguish, we are Greta Garbos who want to be alone and then complain that no one comes to call. The deep mystery of our God is his willingness to be present to us even when we are absent to him. "Before they call, I will answer; and while they are yet speaking, I will hear."[7]

THIS WAY TO FOREVER

Before us there is a whirlwind, and in the midst of the whirlwind is I Am. I Am to whom all the world yearns; I Am, who yearns for his people with a boundless love. I Am is the one who drives all loves, who guides all paths, who walks before us on the yellow brick and every other road. I Am will give us the heart, the mind, the sense of being full, not hollow, who will satisfy all our yearnings and bring us home at last.

His city is more than emeralds, more than sapphire and rubies; all perfection reigns there. In that city the falsehood of our perfectionism is burned away by the fire of God's enduring love. Perhaps it is true that Dorothy Gael is a child deformed by the old child-rearing methods that seek to break her heart and her will. Yet our God is no such heartbreaker. Ours is no hard taskmaster who tries to break the will of the child; instead, he is a tender father who holds his child in a lap of love, waiting, with infinite patience, for the child's free surrender to grace.

Such is the gentle dialogue between the old one and the child; between a Lord who has always lived, has lived and will live forever, and shares his forever with us. We who are made in his image are also incredibly old; if not eternal, we have nevertheless been present in his mind for a very long time, if not surely from the beginning. In any event the Lord has always longed for us; he has lived for us and looked forward eagerly to our response.

So we are someone, after all. We are not orphans, sent on a long journey into Kansas to an Aunty Em who fails to meet the train; we are not the Dorothy whose fairy-tale clothes are snatched from her by abusive adults with bristles of contempt and pain; we are not unwanted children, left on doorsteps by a God who failed to practice birth control.

Our Lord is the one who loved Ephraim when he was a child. He leads us, too, with leading strings of love; he pacifies us with the breast of his tenderness; he stoops down to us, dandles us, presses us to his cheek. Even our sexuality and its transgressions he understands and forgives. *Adonai, Adonai...* even in the violent and lawless cities your name is praised: there and here and everywhere you are truly God.

CHAPTER FIVE

Watches of the Night

MY COUSIN CELESTE HAS SENT ME A GROUP of old photographs and souvenirs from the Mischler-Dietrich family. These are my father's people.

I am unprepared for the emotions I feel as the photographs slip out of the package: waves of memory and not a little pain. Here is my grandfather who died in 1963. In the photograph he is beaming. I remember him smiling over the head of foam on a stein of beer at Kolb's German restaurant. I remember him picking up my mother and father in his shiny black Studebaker as he gives them a ride downtown to work. I remember him fishing in his pocket, almost every day, to give me a bright silver dime or even a quarter to put in my piggy bank. *Where is he now?*

Through the tunnel of memory comes a remembrance of my grandmother Christine, known as Teen or Teenie to the family. She stands at the top of the steps at the house on Dublin Street; the screen door bangs as I go up for my weekly Sunday afternoon visit.

"How are you, kid?" she greets me. She is wiping her hands on her apron. We sit on the front porch and try to talk, but there is almost nothing to say. She calls my grandfather from inside the house. He is asthmatic, often using the breathing machine. I am sixteen, seventeen: it is hard for me to grasp what it is to become old.

My uncle Oliver joins us on the porch. His eyes crinkle with delight when he sees me. Oliver is baffling, an enigma: intelligent, educated, speculative; yet as far as I can see he has no work, no calling, can't sustain a career. What is the affliction that has wounded him? There is a rumor that his life was destroyed by an unhappy love affair, that he has had an emotional crack-up; it is not fitting for a teenager to know about these things, let alone raise questions. Clearly, however, Oliver is a weight on my grandmother's heart.

To me, Teen seems flinty-hard; yet I know she is passionately involved with God. She is intensely Lutheran. My grandfather has left the Roman Catholic church for her sake, a perilous risk to take in the understanding of those days. He must have loved her dearly to take such a step.

Out of the box of Mischler family photographs come still more treasures: rolled up papers of great value. Teen's high school diploma, her confirmation certificate, in German; their marriage certificate, beautifully adorned with Biblical citations. *They have died. They have gone to another place. Where is it? Will I see them again, ever?*

My faith tells me that they stand before God now and their faces are filled with light.

Teen and E.G., Oliver and his wife Doris, all are buried in one of those old New Orleans cemeteries where the tombs are white and beautiful and above ground. I have a photograph of my father, standing in front of the Mischler tomb, remembering Teen and missing her. No doubt he is also contemplating his own life and death. Everyone has such moments, walking through graveyards, confronting the mystery of existence.

IN SURE AND CERTAIN HOPE

It is hard to think of a graveyard as an entrance way to the kingdom; it is hard to think of a grave as the door. Yet from others, people of faith who went before me, I have learned somehow to believe in resurrection. On my mother's side, the family burying-ground is at Grace Church in the small, historic Louisiana town of St. Francisville. I experience a hint of resurrection there. And others who know the place tell me the same: for them it is a place of blessing and peace.

In my mind's ear I hear the voice of the clergyman reciting the Anglican burial service: "In sure and certain hope of the resurrection on the last day, when the final trump shall sound...."

I find myself reliving my own history with this church. All my life, in my visits here, Nui and Eula and my cousins Henry and Anna Prescott have been preparing me for the end of their lives and for the end of my own.

The year is 1982. My son Henry is twelve, but not too young to be one of the pallbearers for Eula's casket. I see how he has a sense of the occasion; being part of the group with other men of the family is a rite of passage for him; he has a sense of ceremony. At her death, Eula is ninety-two. It is a good long life, a life to be celebrated. She has told me on many occasions, "I've had a wonderful life."

Strength of spirit is hard to describe, easy to recognize. It can be felt, it is something substantial. Eula and Nui had it; they knew how to share it. I always thought the Bible had something to do with it. They believed that the Lord was an ever present help in trouble. He would deliver them from the noisome pestilence. They would be strengthened and rescued by his constant vigilance. They would be raised up on eagle's wings.

The spring tea at St. Anna's residence for the elderly is held in 1993 on April 22. On that same day my mother is honored at the Board of Trade, in a beautiful reception for the people of the tourism industry. Because she can't attend two events in one day (her energy is flagging) my mother delegates me to attend the St. Anna's tea. Lalita will be expecting us.

The day is over-scheduled. David Bendix and I are rehearsing and revising our presentation for Helen's party at the Board of Trade. We finish our rehearsal and preparations close to 2 P.M., the starting time of the St. Anna's tea. By the time I get there it is past two o'clock, and I look too much like a business executive, too little like a party guest.

When I go in, Lalita is nowhere to be found. They've taken her upstairs already, I learn. When I pursue her, up the back elevator, I see at last what has been causing my mother's sadness for the past several weeks. Lalita, frail and very old as she is, has been hurt. Her face is black and blue. Her physical injury, on this day, is as nothing to the loneliness she feels.

"I had to come upstairs," she says. "It was terrible. There was a tea and nobody came. Winston didn't come. Helen didn't come."

After a long time I was able to convince her that I had come in Helen's behalf. After a still longer time she realized who I was.

"Emilie! You're Emilie!" Her face was suddenly alight, in spite of the bruises, her beautiful spirit shining through. "How is Helen, how are the children? Tell me about Lucy, Henry, Sarah. Did you get some sandwiches? Go downstairs again, there are lovely refreshments. I'll wait for you."

Weeks later, three days after her ninety-ninth birthday, Lalita dies. "She was ready to go any time," Helen reminds me. But Helen's heart is also breaking that she was not able to go and visit at the last because of her own injuries and infirmity. What sense does it make? What is it all about?

"The coffin will be closed," Petty assures me. Petty is Lalita's niece, she is eighty-five and must move around in a wheelchair. But when I get to the funeral home, the coffin is not closed. The way things are done these days, Lalita seems only to be asleep, looking beautiful, almost smiling. She seems at peace.

But I am filled with sorrow. Not because Lalita has died, it was good for her to die after such times of weakness, impairment, and suffering. For more than a decade she has been completely bent over with severe arthritis. It was time!

I am saddened by the separation. Where is she, when will I see her again? Why does my imagination fail to grasp the passage through the pearly gates? St. Peter in his gown, with his feathery wings in a thousand or so New Yorker cartoons, has weakened my religious imagination. Michelangelo's ceilings, his putti, will not do it for me.

Are Eula and Nui and Lalita in Grace Churchyard? Where is this place they have gone? I stand, a child before a solemn mystery, a riddle to which there is no answer, the riddle through which, as Emily Dickinson says, "sagacity must go."

For a time when our family lived in New York City in the Borough of Queens our apartment overlooked Maple Grove Cemetery. "Doesn't that bother you?" people would say. It didn't bother us; Maple Grove is not anonymous, no overcrowded metropolitan burying-ground. In Maple Grove I often experienced peace. From our apartment window we saw birds, trees, snowfalls, gravestones. On certain days it was part of our walk to the subway. On this walk I once wrote a poem called "Faith."

> It is as though
> in the haze over Queens
> and the sun blazing through it
> I could see the face of God.
> As though in the blooms
> of rhododendron-bushes
> (albeit choked with empty cans)
> I could adore Him.
>
> Even the graves
> as I pass
> shout to me
> God is Life,
> and there is grace
> scattered along my path
> as I reach for the subway-token
> in my pocket.

All efforts to imagine death and the afterlife fail, leaving us feeling foolish and confused. It is simply beyond us; there is, as the Victorian writers used to say, a veil beyond which we cannot see.

I am gripped by a fear, suddenly, that all religious storytelling in the world is delusionary. The moment in the Oz story, when Dorothy and her friends find the little man behind the curtain, pretending to be a great wizard, come back to me. Even the words, in all their whimsy and humor, float back: "Pay no attention to that man behind the curtain." How, then, am I to be comforted? Consolation is a human invention, meant to lull us past our fears!

Is death an illusion? A passage into a new dimension? Is it possible, as some used to suppose, that a vast company of the blessed looks back toward us, rooting for us, praying for us, encouraging us in our struggles? In Thornton Wilder's play, *Our Town*, those who have already died sit on folding chairs to represent a graveyard. They comment on and understand our struggle but they are beyond it; they have moved, as it were, to another level of consciousness, where the things we bleed for no longer matter. When Emily, the central figure of the play, dies and joins them, she is young. She has, perhaps, not let go fully of the attitudes of her former life, she has not fully embraced the life to come. "You know as well as I do," Wilder's Stage Manager explains, "that the dead don't stay interested in us living people for very long. Gradually, gradually... they lose hold of the earth... and the ambitions they had... and the things they suffered... and the people they loved. They get weaned away from the earth—that's the way I put it— weaned away. And they stay here while the earth part of them burns away, burns out; and all that time they slowly get indifferent to what's going on in Grover's Corners. They're waitin'. They're waitin' for something that they feel is comin'. Something important, and great."[1]

Wilder's theology is shaky. He says they are waiting for "the eternal part in them to start coming out." Where is the blazing light of God, lighting up every crevice of those who have gone before us? His insight is animated, perhaps, by belief, but something less than biblical. Emily Dickinson comes closer when she peeks through sagacity's riddle:

> At last to be identified!
> At last, the lamps upon thy side,
> The rest of life to see!
> Past midnight, past the morning star!
> Past sunrise! Ah! What leagues are there
> Between our feet and day![2]

THEY HAVE GONE AHEAD OF US

There are days when those who have died and gone before me speak so strongly to me it is as if they were beside me in the room, like Clarence the angel in a Jimmy Stewart movie, trying to earn his wings. The intimacy of my relationship to my grandmother seems to grow now with each passing year. I think of Eula strongly on certain days, at certain times. Recently I stumbled on a voice recording of Eula and two cousins of mine, Cornelia Cabral and her daughter, Cornelia Quinn, visiting in Helen's living room about family stories and history. To hear their voices, all speaking together, was startling. Two of the four have already died. Yet they were so alive! I thought, now they are even more alive than that.

Growing older is having others die around us; they are our friends, part of ourselves. They have gone ahead to a destiny that is also waiting for us. Yet when we look with eyes of faith it seems these people who have died and gone ahead of us have become more intensely alive, more real. Our lives are bound to theirs with hoops of steel and with mystical cords of flame.

> They are all gone into the world of light
> And I alone sit lingering here.
> Their very memory is fair and bright,
> And my sad thoughts doth clear.

Henry Vaughan's poem is on fire with belief in the more intensified life of those who have gone ahead of him:

> I see them walking in an air of glory,
> Whose light doth trample on my days:
> My days, which are at best but dull and hoary,
> Mere glimmering and decays.

Vaughan goes further. He speaks of Death as something beautiful.

> Dear, beauteous Death! The jewel of the just,
> Shining nowhere, but in the dark;
> What mysteries do lie beyond thy dust,
> Could man outlook that mark!

For Vaughan, death is a liberation. Our intense starlike identities are captured now in a prison of sorts; but death will release them.

> If a star were confin'd into a tomb,
> Her captive flames must needs burn there;
> But when the hand that locked her up gives room,
> She'll shine through all the sphere.[3]

How different from the pagan notion of eternal life! For the Greeks and Romans the immortality of the soul was something endless but not always satisfying. The story of Tithonus, who asked the gods for eternal life, but failed to ask for eternal youth, is a case in point. With their usual enjoyment of human misery, the gods of Olympus granted his wish without rectifying his oversight. Tithonus grew older and older; his immortality was burdensome. At last, he was so aged that his voice became a squeak. In the end, the gods took pity on him and changed him into a cricket!

By contrast, we believers look forward to transformation, a change that begins here and continues hereafter. The New Jerusalem is one vision of this fulfillment. Since childhood I have loved this imagery in the book of Revelation. Mahalia Jackson makes it vivid when she sings about a vision of the Holy City. *Jerusalem, Jerusalem, lift up your gates and sing!* More naïve visions come in the songs of Gospel churches and spirituals of times gone by: *Who's that yonder, dressed in red; must be the Israelites that Moses led; who's that yonder, dressed in white? Must be the people of the Israelite.*

When I myself wanted to trace a vision of the kingdom, I used the small Louisiana town of St. Francisville as my poetic figure. The vision came to me, as you might say, mystically, or at any rate, through a breakthrough in understanding. Like Sook, who understood that the Lord's presence is already with us, in the things we already love, I came to see the presence of God in this small country village so dear to my elders.

St. Francisville was not "the church in the wildwood, so dear to my childhood," as the hymn has it. Instead, it was the place of mystical childhood, more akin to the "joy" that C.S. Lewis speaks of in his memories of childhood wonder. This mystical place, St. Francisville, had been revealed to me by the storytelling of the old people I first loved. Through them, I thought I could re-enter the past, and find a door to heaven along the country path.

"Tell me the story again about twisting the wild horse's tail."

And they would tell me again.

"Tell me the one about Billy and the rattlesnake."

And they would tell me again.

So that when I wanted to spin the vision of a place of perfection, of resolution and completeness, I could hardly find a better place than St. Francisville.[4]

The novelist Walker Percy contributed to the metaphor as well. For him St. Francisville was also a special place, one with memories and meanings. "St. Francisville is an enclave, you know," he said, teasing me about whether I could be buried in the Episcopal cemetery after deciding to embrace Roman Catholic faith. Since he himself had made a similar passage, the joke, he seemed to think, was not only on me but also on him.

People who live in St. Francisville bristle when you tell them it's an enclave. Maybe it isn't, anymore, but Walker Percy was not wrong in remembering its exclusiveness, its clannishness, its small-town just-us-folksness, and a high romanticism about who our people used to be. All this, I saw, would be part of my religious vision of the elect. St. Francisville was the perfect place to symbolize the heavenly kingdom.

Especially when I could use Huey Long's campaign song, "Every Man a King," to tease the idea that in the resurrected life we are all to become priests, prophets, and kings.

After my grandmother's death I wrote two poems. One of them described the arrival of the funeral cortège at the town of St. Francisville.

HOMECOMING

When we came to Alexander's Creek
I thought
she's home now.
And when you said, turn there,
that's the way to Troy,
I thought of her
running, as a child,
no shoes on,
grass between her toes,
twisting the wild horse's tail.

We were all home, then.
But she most of all
having gone home
a whole day ahead of us
long before we came
to Alexander's Creek.

People who pray a great deal find that the boundary between here and hereafter grows thin, like that kind of theatrical curtain called a scrim. This almost transparent drop-sheet reveals a new scene behind the scene which is already illuminated downstage; it creates the effect of an epiphany, a revelation. Now we are like members of the audience who see only what is downstage; later, or when our consciousness is heightened through intimacy with the Lord, we will see beyond the muslin curtain the blessed who have gone before us, and they are about to break into the opening number of the show.

A song from the Broadway musical, *Gypsy*, tells us we are headed for stardom; we have nothing to hit but the heights. Another moment in the theater which always strikes me as a metaphor of heaven comes in the show *Chorus Line*. Throughout this musical, characters are seen mostly in rehearsal clothes. As they tell the story of their personal ambitions and struggles, they are speaking also of a dream of perfection which can't be achieved here and now. In the closing number, which is really a curtain call, all cast members return, now in glittering attire; in top hats they execute the most difficult and dazzling numbers. This is a fore-taste of bliss. "Then we shall know even as now we are known."[5]

OUR NEED FOR METAPHOR

The religious imagination is the way over and through the baf-flement that lies ahead. In a time of great sophistication we reject the imagery our ancestors wove; it is too naïve, too simple-minded, too storybook for us.

Yet metaphors are needed. The Lord speaks to his own in every age and breathes into them the inspiration they need. By intimacy with God we are lighted up; an illumination lets us see the ancient metaphors as speaking to us. Death is a mystery; we can't decipher it; we do not know what we shall be. But we know death as a corollary of time, and we know that even that time we think is given to us is not guaranteed.

Reason enough to live in the present moment, dwelling in the presence of God, treasuring the instant we have against the trials still to come; but faith that moves mountains is greater than this. Genuine faith knows that the times to come are all prefigured in the moment that is. Experience scatters like raindrops across the pane; prayer unifies yesterday, tomorrow, and today. It is time to yield to the structure of experience, to accept the reality of time. Wanting to be masters of the clock, the calendar, lords of the universe, we resent our situation. Why has no one consulted us about the timetable? Were our proposals and preferences not taken into account? How could the Lord have neglected to ask our opinion about the way he has written the rules?

Surrender, a kind of melting, a necessary yielding to the pattern, begins to change us inwardly, and this is the real pursuit of happiness. Enough of chasing through multiple worlds for power and prestige!

In their simplicity the gracious old challenge us to being rather than doing. They praise God by being who they are, not seeking to justify his affections with a list of accomplishments to date. As we pursue the life-voyage we stop keeping a resumé. Earning a degree seems less important than receiving an accolade; it is time to do less, to accept the thanks being given for what we have already done.

And what if there are no thank-yous? If the birthday cards don't seem to come? For years, not realizing it, I looked for my salvation in the mail room. Letters received were my warrant of real life; then I grasped that I was holding on to one more delusionary satisfaction, one more earthly treasure that ought not to be laid up on earth. "Where your treasure is, there will your heart be also."[6]

Fear is the enemy, stalking me in the night. Helen's friend Dorothy is losing her sight. What if I lose mine also? A great scholar at a nearby university, someone I have known since my youth, has gone blind and must be assisted to give his classes by graduate students who help him to walk and consult his notes. How would I manage in such a case? Out of the past, the figure of John Milton, writing epics in spite of blindness, dominates my imagination. I think of Beethoven's deafness. I dream of Einstein's life work.

Does ambition have me in its grip? Do I work to serve or in pursuit of that seducer known as Fame? Why must I write the great American something? Is this not also a failure to trust in the providence of God? Yes, I have to earn a living. But do I have to earn salvation as well? No, it is mine as a gift.

Trust is the issue once again. What kind of a God are we dealing with? Yahweh, I know you are near, standing ever at my side. You guard me from the foe and you lead me in ways everlasting.

CHAPTER SIX

A Different Wisdom

ONE OF THE BEST AND HARDEST THINGS about spiritual life is the way it opens me up to the cross. It isn't so much that I choose the cross. Instead, the cross chooses me. The edge of reality pushes in and I know how powerless I am. I am vulnerable. There are things to face that I want to run away from. Something is asked of me that is more than I can handle, it demands more strength than I have.

The cross is the beginning of a different wisdom: seeing the world from Jesus' point of view. And that can happen most any time if we are open to it. Sometimes though, a spiritual exercise, a walking-on-purpose with the Lord, helps me to share the cross in ways I don't anticipate or plan.

C.S. Lewis puts it well: "The cross comes before the crown, and tomorrow is a Monday morning."[1] Sometimes it is in the sheer Mondayness of things that I experience the cross. Often in our everyday lives we feel impoverished, pinned down. Even if I have goods and resources, I feel that I'm not really free. Something is binding me, there's an anxiety that cuts straight through everything, reminding me that things are out of whack. It's partly my own weakness, but it's everyone else's too. There's the weariness of putting one foot in front of the other, not to mention some other "slings and arrows of outrageous fortune." Someone I know is dying of AIDS. Still another friend who dies "wills me" his loneliness. I realize he died almost friendless and alone. All around me are signs of limitation: boundaries I didn't wish for and can't change. There is no way out but straight ahead. Liberation sounds like an empty word unless Christ is the way.

Oddly, it is freeing to enter into the story. With Christ, in Christ, I can pass into a deeper reality, but only when I am willing to make the walk to Calvary myself. I like that passage in Isaiah that says the suffering servant wasn't good-looking. "The crowds were appalled on seeing him—so disfigured did he look that he seemed no longer human."[2] It's hard to recognize a Savior when he's powerless, worse off than we are. This is the part of reality I don't want to admit to myself, that suffering is the way in. "Without beauty, without majesty (we saw him), no looks to attract our eyes; a thing despised and rejected by men, a man of sorrows and familiar with suffering, a man to make people screen their faces." I have to admit I'm inclined to forget who Jesus is and how to let his sacrifice cut into my life. "He was despised and we took no account of him."[3]

Yet, if I live the story out fully, I also have to be among the soldiers who divided his garments; I have to include the part where I give him vinegar and ask if he is really the King after all. If I'm honest, I have to be all the actors in the drama, playing every role to the hilt. I have to demand that Barabbas be set free instead.

At least this honesty is cleansing; the denial, the whipping, the scourging, the mocking, all are part of my divided self that loves the Lord and denies him, turns around and looks the other way. I have to be both Judas and Peter. When I'm living the story I'm also feeling the rejection Jesus felt. "By force and by law he was taken; would anyone plead his cause? Harshly dealt with, he bore it humbly, he never opened his mouth, like a lamb that is led to the slaughterhouse, like a sheep that is dumb before its shearers."[4]

In my own life, it is sometimes clear that the more Christ is with me the less I am a comfortable person to know. My simple choice to belong to Christ may bind me to some people but it separates me from others. That is part of what hurts about the Christian life; we don't ever fully "fit in." When I am in the marketplace I can't escape noticing this difference. Really living as a Christian, I don't always feel better but worse, because the prevailing culture exerts such a pull. Even when others don't understand me, I have to love them anyhow, doing my part to help them feel at ease with me! If I live my life unself-consciously I might be doing good. I can even forget about it. Then some chance remark reminds me I'm walking by a different path, making commitments that others find hard to handle. One interesting twist to this experience is those unbelieving friends of mine who love me even when they don't grasp my commitment to faith. This is a kind of trust for them as well.

Yet the surprise of this trip to Calvary is that there's something at the end of the road besides death and suffering. I can't seem to get there by applying a theory of the cross. "By his stripes we are healed" has a practical meaning. But I have to follow, one step at a time, to sense that there is something else in store. Just when I think the glory of the resurrection is very unlikely, I find myself standing in the garden with Mary Magdalene after all. Suddenly, where I least expect it, he is alive and calling me by name. "Jesus said, 'Mary!' She knew him then and said to him in Hebrew, 'Rabbuni,' which means Master. Jesus said to her, 'Do not cling to me, because I have not yet ascended to the Father. But go and find the brothers, and tell them.'"[5]

As unlikely as it seems, we do find him in the moment as Mary did or the disciples on the Emmaus Road. We see him in the stranger at table, in the chance meeting, in the love that floods our hearts, yet causes pain. The Lord seems closer when we stop pretending to be powerful and admit how wounded we are. Then he seems to come to us, crucified and risen. When we are honest in prayer, the Lord can catch and embrace us, he can hold us tight. We touch him. We grasp him. To this real Master we cling, this vulnerable Lord with the wounds still open in his hands and side.

A HARSHER TRUTH

It used to be commonplace to talk about our "crosses," the trials and burdens of everyday living we couldn't walk away from or forget. The phrase was, "We all have little crosses to bear." But becoming open to the cross is somewhat different from that. This is the tension that seems to split existence in two. At moments we sense it. We recognize the harsher truth that underlies everything. It is an invitation, yet one we're not so eager to accept.

When we surrender, we too are marked with the painful tension that scars all reality. The world is maimed, distorted, out of whack. The time, as Hamlet says, is out of joint, not just for one generation but all generations. But Hamlet misses the mark when he supposes he was born to put it right. There is only one who can put it right, and he has already done so, bearing the tension, the division of existence in his body, so to speak. Not just at Easter, but always, the mystery is played out in history as one, once-for-all event: the Son pouring out his blood for the Father and for us, sending the Spirit to bind and heal us once and for all.

I think we grasp this reconciliation for ourselves only when we are willing to undergo the cross, not just romantically but practically in the way we live. Are we shouting too much? Drinking too much? Giving way to the peer-demands and pressures around us? Just ahead is the path we should be walking, the footprints painfully clear. Are we walking with him, yielding to what he asks?

Or are we forgetting, denying, not living for him but living for number one?

Some days in the Christian calendar are chances for a change of direction. They prompt us to a specific glimpse of Jesus Christ.

> Across the littered streets
> falls the long shadow of the cross;
> And over the Manhattan sky
> I see his face
> Thrown back in suffering.

My own poem, written several Good Fridays ago, reminds me of how I can touch the Lord in the pain and poverty of city places.

> Just beyond me
> A small procession
> Moves through Jerusalem streets.
> I too am on my way to Calvary.

How am I living the cross? If I can't feel the edge of it in my consciousness, then the fullness of reality is lacking. I need to lean into the whirlwind of his presence, assent to the storm he stirs up in me. I have to relent and die with him to be sure of knowing how to be alive. I have to open my heart, my consciousness, to see him, crucified, changing the meaning, transforming the event. There, just beyond the cross, in the sky getting darker hour by hour, I can see the outline of the universe, God designing everything, and us, for himself, to be swept up into his flaming heart.

Is the way narrow? How are we supposed to enter in? We do it by consenting, leaning into the particular, feeling the nails in our hands.

> Do not weep for me, daughters of Jerusalem.
> He knows the outcome.

> Master, how can I thank you for this gift? This depth

of vision that lets me live your story, knowing it as my own? Do I value enough the pearl of your existence? Of knowing how to walk to Calvary with you?

How can I deal with the mystery that is Easter, the death that calls us to live? In the surrender of one man the broken pieces of existence are made whole again.

GIFTS FROM THE SEA

I write this from mid-ocean, not knowing my way. My directions are unclear. My supplies are running short. Darkness is darkness. I know what it means to be at sea.

I can't help thinking that an experience of darkness can never be fully staged. We can't really orchestrate an experience of emptiness; it's not a matter of chosen hardships or fasting. Wilderness is always impromptu, a gift that comes out of nowhere, without rehearsal or warning. When a real desert experience sets in, there's no time to prepare. We're up against it. Trapped in a place without comfort, without support.

Things that fed us before don't seem to nourish us now. Who are we? Where are we going? Why don't the plans and dreams we had yesterday add up? Isn't there a structure, a design we can cling to? The map doesn't match the circumstances. We're going in circles, exhausted, lost. Now's the time to grumble, to tell Moses and Aaron they've betrayed us. This experience isn't play-acting. The lines we memorized don't work for these situations. "Why did we not die at Yahweh's hand in the land of Egypt?... As it is, you have brought us to this wilderness to starve the whole company to death!"[6] As so often, when dealing with God, he seems to have changed the rules. We're inclined to tell him he's not playing fair. "Why did you bring us out of Egypt?... Was it so that I should die of thirst, my children too, and my cattle?"[7]

WISDOM COMES WHEN WE LOOK BACK

It's only after the fact that a desolate experience can be seen as a gift. In the middle of it our vision is dim. We can't see past the present moment. The main response that comes to mind is a howl. This alienation isn't a spiritual exercise that can be scheduled when it's convenient. It rarely seems to coincide with our plans. God's unpredictability is a constant. Now, the question is: how can I get out of this? How can I be glad the spiritual life is never boring?

Maybe the Israelites' story has its own answer coded in. The manna that was sent was barely enough for each day's need, no grace left over for the day to come. (He did send an extra supply to tide them over the Sabbath.)

Each day's anxiety has to be lived in trust. That's theory, not practice. Are the shortages meant for my growth? I can't see it. (My gravest temptation is to stage-manage everything, write the script, and demand that God play his assigned role.) Instead, I need to hold on minute by minute. The more we hold on, give in, the more the actual moment hollows us out. By a gift of imagination, we endure; we grope; we tough it through. "We do not know where you are going, Lord. So how shall we know the way?"[8]

In the blush of my first enthusiasm for the spiritual life, I once wanted to take on penances and deliberately chosen fasts. Then my spiritual director counseled me wisely: "Better the penance that you don't choose." Now that I have come into such a place, a place not of my own choosing, it is painful even to remember the false heroics of my earlier plan.

In the past I volunteered to help those who had to stay put. As a lay minister in my New York congregation, I became a regular Sunday visitor to nursing homes. In a sense I think I was trying to compensate for the ways I couldn't be attentive to my own family, living far away. Whatever my intention, I saw a lot of anguish, people trapped in loneliness with less than adequate care.

Yes, it was a generous act; yes, it was worth doing. But some of that overenthusiastic ministry seems to me now less than holy, an effort to take center stage in a publicly Christian way.

How much better to stay put and stand toe-to-toe with my own challenges. Now I am fenced in as they were; now it's not so easy to voice my Christian enthusiasm. Now I can't romanticize the experience of tending the sick. Now I see that I am not "caring for the elderly" but becoming one of the elderly for whom others must care. My impulse is to make a break for freedom, for irresponsibility, to cut loose from being the good, obedient child.

Living the cross is giving ourselves when we have nothing to give: breaking, for a moment, the whine of the TV, the drone of conversation behind the hospital curtain. This is an unidentified location somewhere between Horeb and Sinai. We live in hope that tomorrow's manna will fall, as promised.

I know it is time to drop all my disguises, the ways I hide from God. "Down in the dust I lie prostrate: revive me as your word has guaranteed.... I have chosen the way of fidelity, I have set my heart on your rulings. I cling to your decrees."[9] A new role has been assigned to me; one that gives me a chance to be vulnerable, open, naked, needy, loving, trusting, hour by hour, day by day. Whatever time of year it comes, this is my Lent, an undressing, a stripping off of assumed and false identities. In another sense it is also its own drama or play: our acting-out of Jesus' ordeal in the wilderness. Putting on Christ, as Paul says, is dressing up to be like our Lord.

I am called to walk through times of confusion and doubt, playing a new part—the faithful Jewishness of Jesus. Or, at the very least, keeping my eyes fixed on the Jesus who walks just ahead. Time to ask again, Who is this man? What is he calling me to? And why do we care about him so? "You did not see him, yet you love him; and still without seeing him, you are already filled with a joy so glorious that it cannot be described, because you believe; and you are sure of the end to which your faith looks forward.... It was this salvation that the prophets were looking and searching so hard for; their prophecies were about the grace which was to come to you."[10] How can we grow beyond our fears in the aging process? Only perhaps by yielding to that experience and keeping a sharp eye for God's guiding presence: angelic sentinels and guardians can protect us from ourselves, our own deepest fears and anxieties, our continuing fear of change.

THE PULL OF THE FUTURE

As the nineties advance we can almost feel the century turning; the future pulls us mightily on. We pray for a political and spiritual awareness that can befriend us in uncertain times with ways to interpret present, past, and future. We hope for perspectives to help us look a hundred years in both directions: where we have come from, where we are going after a century of accelerating change in knowledge and thought. We want to connect with the past and future in a continuum of belief. We want to be like Einstein's "observer" and his time traveller who by moving at the speed of light remains young.

Those who in their lifetimes have spanned the cold war, lived through Christian religious realignments, watched Eastern and Western coalitions re-emerge, may come to the close of the century rather weary. We wonder whether political and social change is merely cyclic, fearing that when things change, they only stay the same. Young and old, we need hope, curiosity, wonder; we want to plunge into new quandaries with fresh zeal. The emergence of spirit in many zones, the stacking of consciousness upon consciousness, worldwide planetary anxieties that well may unify the human race—all these things have brought to the forefront religious concerns that at mid-century were often dismissed as beside the point. Once again, it is the best of times and the worst of times, the age of incredulity and the age of belief. Clinging to the Word and the work will hold us steady through sea-changes that lie ahead, long after the printing press is a memory and our whole history has been converted to a computer chip.

"Growing older is a phenomenon which is a common denominator for all of us," writes Sister Marie Lenihan, CSJ, who has devoted many years of her life to work with older persons. "As one enters the latter years of life, activity becomes less possible and the scope of our lives more limited. We come face to face with the reality of our own dying process."

And living process!

"Those of us who have the tremendous privilege," she continues, "of continued contact with people who are now in the frail stages of life, can see their virtues. We see their centeredness in God, their resourcefulness of facing life's difficulties, their emotional maturity and ability to view situations with a positive outlook. Each person develops these characteristics to a greater or lesser degree because of his or her life experiences, choices made, and personality makeup. Many persons at this stage in life have wisdom that only life experience can bring, and a faith that can strengthen and support those around them.

"These qualities sustain the people as they grow older."[11]

Consider a poet who in old age became still more visionary: Alfred Lord Tennyson. Like us he felt the pull of the millennium, an end-of-the-century magnetism. In his mind's eye the future held great wonders as well as great uncertainties. Closer in spirit to us, perhaps, than any other generation of believers are our nineteenth-century cousins of the spirit and the heart. Tennyson, in his eighty-first year, not long before his death, wrote about the last passage in high nautical style.

> Sunset, and evening star
> And one clear call for me
> And may there be no moaning of the bar

When I put out to sea.
But such a tide as moving seems asleep,
Too full for sound and foam,
When that which drew from out the boundless deep
Turns again home.
Twilight and evening bell
And after that the dark!
And may there be no sadness of farewell,
When I embark;
For though from out our bourne of Time and Place
The flood may bear me far,
I hope to see my Pilot face to face
When I have crossed the bar.[12]

In a memoir, Tennyson explained who the Pilot was: "that Divine and Unseen Who is always guiding us." A few days before his death, Tennyson asked that this poem be printed at the end of all editions of his poems. For me it has in it the sound of the evening bell, telling the time at sea, insistently, as the vessel moves into the dark.

CHAPTER SEVEN

Lands of Nod

C AN THIS LAST LIFE-PASSAGE LEAD US into new creativity and playfulness? When the heavy obligations of our forties and fifties drop away, can we explore reality in a new way? Can we let go of the anxiety of parenthood?

"You're down-nesting," my son Henry explains, as my husband and I outline what we think we may want to do with the house for the future. There is a possibility that my mother may move in; it's clear that Henry already has moved out, but without letting go of his collecting privileges and without fully vacating his room. We want him to stay; but we must renegotiate our relationships as adults. His devotion as a son is part of what sustains us and gives us hope; we want to see a lot of him, for the fun of his presence and his light conversation. How would we decide what films to see if we couldn't consult him? How would we know what novels by younger and established writers are worth reading?

The relationship we have to our own parents (the Griffins are both gone; my father is gone, only my mother remains) has the same substance and frailty as the golden cord that links us to Lucy,

Henry, and Sarah. They are imaginative, loving, lively, creative; they know one day we too will be gone. They watch us grow old before their eyes; our limbs are stiffer; we complain of new ailments; we are obsessed with our work, with completing the task. Clearly we are in a difficult transition. They stand helplessly by, not knowing what to do, laughing with us, encouraging us, pointing out our failings in joking fashion. Birthday cards, gifts, loans, patience, favors of one sort or another, these are the ways they show their love. We know we are rich in having their affections, seeing their achievements, sharing their hopes, friendships, aspirations, even their sadness, their losses, their confusion.

"What are Helen's ancestors doing in our living room?" With this startling question Henry revealed to me ten years ago that he had not yet accepted his Southern past. As these aristocratic white slaveholders looked down from the walls, the women with their Spanish combs, black bombazine dresses, camellias in their laps, the men with crisp white Wordsworthian collars and noses red from a London night out on the town (not to mention Sarah Jennings Churchill, first Duchess of Marlborough)... these vestiges of high birth and the painful heritage of the past, have borne down on Henry's sensitive conscience as they did on mine. How can we come to grips with our history? How can we deal with the sins of those who did not even recognize their sins?

"White? It means nothing to me. When they say 'I'm Italian,' 'I'm Jewish,' whatever, I get upset because I can't really say what I am. I am an African-American, I'm just a black person in America," says twenty-seven-year-old Robert McGriff, a New Orleans teacher and counselor, interviewed in *The New Orleans Times-Picayune*. "I can't even claim the continent of Africa, because I don't know where exactly I came from. I don't know whether I'm Kenyan, or I'm Zulu. I don't know if I'm from Morocco. I don't know."[1]

We are all the children of God through baptism into Christ Jesus. "There are no more distinctions between Jew and Greek, slave and free, male and female, but all of you are one in Christ Jesus," says the writer to the Galatians.[2] He goes on to explain the adoption as sons that we have all experienced through Christ Jesus. "The proof that you are sons is that God has sent the Spirit of his Son into our hearts: the Spirit that cries "Abba, Father," and it is this that makes you a son, you are not a slave any more; and if God has made you a son, then he has made you an heir."[3]

The genealogy that should most concern us is our spiritual descent from Abraham and our inclusion in the broad and generous covenant between God and humanity. Yet we worry about who we are and where we have come from, tracing our family histories through the baptismal registers and family Bibles and marriage certificates on the civil rolls.

Is there any harm in it? Surely there is much to praise in the work of hereditary and patriotic organizations, those who build monuments and lay wreaths to remind us of worthy and sometimes forgotten causes. Drenched in family history on my mother's side, where a sense of lost nobility was always somehow lamented, part of the myth, I had to wrestle with my working-class history on my father's side, where few records were kept and hardly a photograph remains. "High birth," Eula quoted to me once, "was ever in the mind." She attributed the saying to King Alfred. Don't we all, on some level, long to believe that we are meant to rule? Our faith tells us that we will come into that inheritance. Royalty is part of the promise, not a human royalty that is subject to losses, rivalries, conspiracies, political whims, but a royalty of the spirit that can never pass away, a royalty that is possible to anyone who is faithful to the promise he or she receives.

STORYTELLING GIVES US HOPE

Perhaps the best thing about family storytelling is the way that myths are spun, myths that commemorate the betrayals of the past, the chicanery, the double-dealing, and myths that exalt our forebears for their courage in adversity. In each family there are patriarchs, who, like Moses and Aaron and Miriam, lead us out of the land of the Pharaohs and out of the house of bondage. For my mother, my grandmother, for Eula and Julia, these patriarchal figures were Papa and Mamma. If they had human failings, we never heard about them. Instead we heard how they won in perilous times through strength of character and the capacity for hope. I tried to capture this thematic storytelling in three prose poems.

I

Plantation child
running with fat legs
along the dust brown path,
patting with pink toes
over the bridge,
the creek,
down by the bayou's edge:
you are eighty now, and more.
You hold the needle out,
peer for the thread,
remembering ghosts:
Mamma and Papa and Uncle Sid
and mules to ride on,
pulling the wagon,
turning the gin,
and I look up, listening,
dreamy heart, dreamy eyes,
trying to think it was I,
blackberry pickin'
with black lisle stockings
stretched over my hands.

II

If I had a coat of arms
I would have wisteria,
rampant.

As I first saw it grow
where Mamma's house was:
just a black chimney now.
The fire took it.
Do you know she had king-snakes in the house
as pets?
Only country folk could sleep there,
those who loved wild things, unafraid.
When she was old,
Feltus, the man of all work
who lived on the place,
got the old car to sputter,
drove her into town.
She's gone, and so the house is.
But the wisteria throngs and climbs over the
token-fences.
For what fence could enclose Mamma's wild things?

III

Mamma lived at Troy;
Papa at Forest.
Oh, no, not my Mamma.
My grandmother's Mamma.
Everyone called her that.
I would have, too. But she died.
My grandmother kept her thimble in the sewing-box.
And everyone recalled her.
In the faded albums
She was just an old lady.
Frumpy black dress, stout tummy, practical shoes.
But cameras twist. Photographs betray.
I could trust memories more.
Mamma, who never looked back when the plantation
went.
Not for taxes really.

Something worse, cousin selling cousin
down the river.
Into the land of Pharaoh.
Papa was brave, too.
Everyone said it.
Do we have Papas now that everyone believes in?
God, please let me be like Papa and Mamma.
Your humble servants of Troy and Forest.
Just this I ask in Jesus' name.
Amen.

WEAVING FAMILY RITUALS

One of the possible sources of creativity at this moment in our lives is the conscious weaving of family rituals. No doubt this is part of the parents' desire to hold on to the younger generation; as such it should be carefully questioned and scrutinized. But on another level, our family rituals are part of a desire to pass something on, something precious that exists at the level of memory and story. These are the jewels of our experience that have power to make our children more free.

"In the mid-life transition," say Evelyn and James Whitehead, "an adult may feel drawn inward, toward the pole of separateness."[4] They are drawing on Levinson's interpretation of the work of Carl Jung. Levinson speaks of a mid-life polarity between attachment and separateness. Attachment, for Levinson, is engagement, with career, with the hurly-burly of community affairs, the busy exchanges of living. Separateness is not isolation, but rather a turn toward reflectiveness, one which brings a new creativity to bear on our lives and relationships.

I remember clearly trying to evaluate what was distinctively ours in family life. What would we treasure as the unique voice of our common relationships? How did we celebrate Christmas in a specially Griffin way? I began to treasure, for example, one of Henry Griffin's holiday affectations: that of hiding gifts around the house (perhaps this began in his early childhood with Easter eggs) and then writing humorous clues so that we could find them. Lucy, I noticed, was especially good at planning and writing cards and notes; funny birthday cards seemed to be her signature. Sarah's contribution to family life seemed to come in terms of order; Sarah from the beginning has brought her gifts of social reform into the family circle. When I was unable to make order in the kitchen because of painful work overloads, Sarah began to create the perfect kitchen, at least in her mind's eye. In her neat handwriting I found lists of needed groceries, of spices on hand. Gradually from these clues I began to spin my own conceptions of what might hold our family together in the scattering of our mature lives.

CHRISTMAS: A TIME OF POVERTY

Christmas comes to mind, leaping out at me from the albums, a metaphor of family closeness and also a reproach. In the staged photographs of my own childhood Christmas I know and remember a kind of falsehood: my parents were on the verge of a breakup which the photographs don't show. Our yearning for a Christmas of perfection is a yearning for what is not yet, a something we can dream of but can't fully possess.

The familiar rituals, the lights, decorating, preparation, filled as they are with confrontation and anxiety, are in some ways representative of the feast. Yet we want to live Thanksgiving and Christmas out in a spirit of prayer; the holidays call us to hope that dreams come true.

This year, I experience Christmas months ahead. I have a sharper sense of what the festivities mean. Perhaps it is the loss that I know I am dealing with; the loss of family life as it has been, the casual, unplanned visiting and exchange of conversations, even the buffeting and the arguing have become dear to me.

The reflective spirit turns everything upside down and inside out. Christmas is not a time of lavish bounty but of inner fasting; we are poor and we know it as we wait for the birth of the king. Among the tinsel and the glitter, the catalogs brimming with extravagant options, there is another spirit at work: a spirit of simplicity that wants the power of the manger story to flood our hearts. We want to be open to Christmas, a Christmas that makes sense on a deeper level, in ways we can't explain.

One of the reflective exercises I have pursued and recommended every holiday season is praying Mary's prayer, called The Magnificat, through the four weeks of Advent. This is a historic season of preparation for the birth of the Lord and also for the final coming of Christ. More to the point it asks us to become ready for Christ to enter our hearts. Mary's prayer, prayed throughout the season, helps us to develop mindfulness, a reflective, even a contemplative spirit. It is a prayer said in search of biblical wisdom.

> My soul magnifies the Lord
> And my spirit rejoices in God my savior
> For he that is mighty has done great things for me
> And holy is his name.[5]

When we become fully mindful, as Mary is, both of the power of God and of our own powerlessness, we approach the holy season of Christmas and we understand how much there is in the world that we would change if we could, but which we are powerless to change. We need, fully, to surrender to the Lord's working in our lives, and at the same time, we need fully to hope for the coming of the kingdom here and now.

This kind of prayer, tied to a season, which carries us through and into an event—praying through Advent, toward Christmas, or through Lent, toward Easter and beyond—reminds us of how particular our lives are, how we are creatures of time. By imagination we can become even more connected to reality if we ride with Mary on her journey from Galilee to Bethlehem, waiting to bring the Christ child to birth. When we make such a spiritual journey with vivid imagination, we come across our own impatience. We are faced with a longing to get on with it, to conclude, to arrive somewhere, to know that our time has been well spent, that the time we are spending is not spent in vain.

We want to know what we, who are Mary's people, following in her footsteps, can actually do in our own lives... what we can accomplish against this enormous weight of sadness that we feel. And we want to know how we can adequately bring joy to others, to bring Jesus to birth in our own lives and in the lives of others, in a city and a country torn by violence and exhausted by fear.

What can we do? What can anyone do? We can hope.

Hope is the child that Mary bears. Hope is the child we too can bear, in our thoughts, in our actions, in our lives.

THE POOR ON OUR DOORSTEP

Let me tell you about Myrtle, who comes to our door every Christmas and holiday, looking for a little something. Because of some of the twists of the social structure in the South, I have to believe that even though Myrtle comes to our doorway asking for things, she is not precisely a beggar. Myrtle is a person who believes that the promises made to Israel are true.

Myrtle seems to expect a kind of justice. She supposes that between the people who live on Prytania Street, and the government of the United States, and Kingsley House, and the City of New Orleans, that though she is old and infirm and doesn't have all her own teeth, that everything is going to be all right.

Myrtle is the person the Lord has sent to us to be a vivid

reminder of God's presence in our midst. She announces in a somewhat irritating way (she rings the doorbell very noisily, and with high expectations) that the poor who trust in the mercy of God and in the kindness of their neighbors are under his protection. They are his poor; they are Mary's poor; they are my poor; and I am responsible for them.

Now there is another voice in me that cries out, I am powerless. Myrtle better take care of herself, because I have nothing to give her. Myrtle, for me, is that woman bothering the judge in the middle of the night till he got up and gave her justice.

Myrtle is for me, in Hebrew phrase, the *anawim*, the powerless person in the vast, shredding cloth of society, here and everywhere, that reminds me I must care.

John Baillie, in his book, *Invitation to Pilgrimage*, has this to say: "The Bible everywhere encourages us to believe that those who work for righteousness are allying themselves with his almighty power and can count on his support, while those who work for evil are his enemies and have his power against them."[6]

All through the wars of the Old Testament it is not Israel that is spoken of as winning the battles but God. "Thus God that day humbled Jabin the king of Canaan before the Israelites."[7] After the battle was finished, Deborah proclaimed in song that "the stars in their courses fought against Sisera" who was Jabin's commander in chief. This is, Baillie insists, the oldest piece of Hebrew literature extant, the Book of the Wars of Jehovah.[8]

This theme is pervasive throughout the Old Testament. "Some trust in chariots, and some in horses; but we will remember the name of the Lord our God."[9] "Through you we trampled down our enemies, through your name we subdued our aggressors. My trust was not in my bow, my sword did not gain me victory."[10]

"The Lord of Hosts proclaims, Israelites and Men of Judah are trampled down together; their captors hold them fast and will not let them go. But theirs is a strong champion, his name is the Lord of Hosts; he will take their part, and daunt the Babylonians, that the world may live at peace."[11]

"Except the Lord keep the city, the watchman waketh but in vain."[12] Baillie asks what right the Israelites had, and what right we have to believe that God is on our side. The answer, he solemnly insists, is that "we can count on having God on our side only so far as we are on his. The question is not whether God is allying himself with us, but whether we are allying ourselves with God. But whenever we do ally ourselves with him, we have the full assurance of his providential help."[13]

This abiding hope in the justice of God is what we express when we pray with the mind of Mary. Mary's simplicity and reflectiveness help us to believe, with a serene and childlike confidence, that roses can bloom in December and snow can fall in July. The faith of the simple heart tells us that even the wasted cities can burst into bloom, at Christmas or any other time, for those who are willing to work for the Lord's kingdom and those who are willing to pray.

Do we have this kind of courage? To believe, as Mary did, that God is working in our lives and that he will overshadow us with his enormous power? Are we willing to make Mary's surrender and believe that good things will also happen today for those who are willing to act for God's kingdom now?

Even when we begin to be wounded by the piercing imagery of salvation, something inside of us holds back, a little voice keeps nagging away. What in the world does this time honored, sacred tableau have to do with the way we live now?

In answer to this Thomas-doubt, words of Scripture come to mind:

And it happened that as he was speaking, a woman in the crowd raised her voice and said, "Blessed is the womb that bore you and the breasts that fed you." But Jesus replied, "More blessed still are those who hear the word of God and keep it."[14]

This saying of Jesus reminds us how things really are. What has been nurtured in Mary's womb is our fertility. What Mary labors to give birth to is the Christ who rules in us.

We are somehow the womb, the creative environment in which Christ's meaning can take hold, be nourished in dark places, grow and swell, breaking open at last in ways that can heal and invigorate our lives.

Not so many years ago, a number of us were encouraged by the witness of forty-five recording artists who gathered together to accomplish a miracle for the children of Africa.

Yes, we were disillusioned when much of the huge sum raised was siphoned off by graft and double-dealing.

But in our own immediate neighborhoods, when children are in need, and we can see how interwoven the fabric of our society is, we cannot fail to respond to the needs of God's poor, in Hebrew phrase, the *anawim*. We ourselves, who are powerless, we who are spiritually and materially needy, we who know the pinch of want, we also know the power of the Lord's generosity to us.

Last Christmas I was moved by the knowledge that my friend, Gail Hodges Tranchin, had been diagnosed with cancer. She was told that she had only a few months, perhaps a year to live. The poignancy of Christmas and its celebrations was heightened for me by knowing it was perhaps Gail's last Christmas. With my usual failure to accept the facts realistically, I sensed her frailty and limitations without fully grasping my own.

Our luncheon circle gathered at a downtown hotel. Across the table, my eyes met Gail's now and then. I had known her since fifth grade. I wanted to say something about what this lifelong friendship had meant to me. But I did not. Instead it seemed better to celebrate being together rather than to speak about the future. I am not sure I ever adequately expressed my affection before her death.

But I saved the place card—a little Christmas tree—throughout the long months of the following year. Somehow I was enlivened by her courage, her apparent confidence in the face of death. The small cardboard Christmas tree kept making me think of the holiday brilliance of the Windsor Court Hotel Grill Room, something that made me think of sweetness of friends gathered for the holiday, the circle that will always include Gail.

THE EBB AND FLOW OF TIME

Vita brevis! Life is short, not always sweet. Holidays heighten our sense of the ebb and flow, the boundaries of time. Now our yearning for justice and our sense of being powerless to achieve it is deepened. We must put our trust in Yahweh for all that we aspire to and be grateful to him for all that we are.

In his commentary on Luke, the Scripture scholar Eugene Laverdie summarizes the meaning of the Magnificat in two short paragraphs. Mary, he says, contrasts her humble condition with the greatness of what God has done. Her attention then turns to the extraordinary reversals of divine history in which God's strength and greatness reduce human pride, might, and wealth to no account, exalts those who humbly recognize their position before God, and fills the hungry with good things. Mindful of his merciful love, God thus fulfills his promise to Abraham and his posterity forever.

The canticle, he says, summarizes the themes of Luke and Acts: concern for the poor and politically weak; for Christian leadership which must not assume the ways of human power; for the quality of Christian nourishment (at the Lord's table); and for the fulfillment of God's promise of blessing to Abraham and his true posterity.

When we pray with the mind of Mary, we will understand ourselves as the true posterity of Abraham. In all the books I write I have a simple motive: to celebrate surrender and to announce that biblical things do happen. To vouch for my own experience that God is still attentive, even in the twentieth century, to those of us who pray. I want to use my creative skill to interweave contemporary experience with scriptural understanding, to proclaim, with the mind of Mary, that the fairy tale of our experience with God is true.

Gail is dead now. She has gone to that other place. I must believe by faith in the ending of the fairy tale, that a magnificent glory is in store for her, that she is entering in to her royal inheritance.

"What shall I give him, poor that I am?" Christina Rossetti asks in her nativity poem.[15] Holidays bring home to us how poor we are, how little we have to show for our efforts. As we grow older we come to the manger empty-handed and our eyes are wet.

In the cradle scene I identify less with the wise men than with the shepherds, perhaps most of all with the friendly beasts who have only their own warmth and affection to give. There is nothing of the world's abundance that can enrich this Child we wait for; he comes to give us the treasure of poverty, of spiritual childhood. That's the reversal of values we most need to learn.

We come naked into the world, but it takes time to understand what we really lack. Christmas after Christmas we grasp our own poverty and see in the beggars and the homeless a reminder of how powerless we are. The kingdoms of the world will not satisfy us; this earth as we know it is passing away, and the new Christendom coming to birth has nothing of empire about it. One must be a child to enter in.

We have heard the carols so often that we don't listen to the words. Yet a deep wisdom is hidden in them. The mythmakers embroider the poverty of the king. "No crib for his bed." "No room for him at the inn." "Once in royal David's city." The rightful king who has come is made homeless by a world that can't assess his wealth. Can we do any better? Can we become rich by his counsels of inner poverty? Only if we are children enough to hear the story freshly as though for the first time.

All the more reason for praying, even in a time so rushed and hectic that prayer seems impractical, postponable. In our holiday praying we meet, as Scrooge did, the ghosts of Christmas past, present, and to come. We have to deal with old memories, child-hood recollections of what Christmas used to be, the selves we have outgrown and left behind. That ghost reminds us, too, how much we must hand Christmas on to those who are very young. For their not-always-comprehending sakes we must keep the full meaning of Christmas, even the hard parts. Not just tinsel and glitter, but compassion: forgotten relatives, elderly cousins, needy and forsaken persons too near to be glamorous. And the ghost of Christmas present? That's the one that haunts me with my own fakery, my sudden sense of how little real good I have done. What hearts have I mended? What wounds did I bind up? What quarrels have I soothed? How much have I really loved? And then, forgiving... Have I really tried? There are nettles of unforgiveness, clogging my path.

Just in time, on cue, comes the third ghost, Christmas yet to come. "So live, that when your moment comes to join the eternal caravan...." Not Scripture, but poetry. This ghost will stop at nothing to wound my heart! Like Scrooge, it seems, I have to be converted, just when I thought I had done all the turning I could do. Am I flexible enough for this? And will I have enough reprieve to mend my ways, to send a goose to Bob Cratchit after all? Is the Lord playing fair, really, when he uses my Christmas meditation as a way of calling me again to a deeper conversion of heart? It seems he wants nothing less than for me to become a child again. But how can I become a child when I am old? And what shall I give him, poor that I am?

Holidays have an ache, a yearning. We are at Bethlehem; we would be at Jerusalem.

"I know all about you: how you are neither cold nor hot. I wish you were one or the other, but since you are neither, but only lukewarm, I will spit you out of my mouth. You say to yourself, 'I am rich, I have made a fortune, and have everything I want,' never realizing that you are wretchedly and pitiably poor, and blind and naked too."[16]

We are called again to walk the hard path, to keep Christmas on a level deeper than the storybooks. Time is the bell ringer. The Lord himself is the path we walk on, the peace we are hoping for. Where and what is home for us who have no place to lay our heads? Holidays remind us that we have no home, no resting place except in God.

What child is this who laid to rest on Mary's lap is sleeping? Before the manger, among the friendly beasts, with our own children or without them, we know the Child is for us. "I warn you, buy from me the gold that has been tested in the fire to make you really rich, and white robes to clothe you and cover your shameful nakedness.... I am the one who reproves and disciplines all those he loves: so repent in real earnest."[17]

By prayer we know we are the needy children starving for grace. "Look, I am standing at the door, knocking. If one of you hears me calling and opens the door, I will come in to share his meal, side by side with him.... If anyone has ears to hear, let him listen."[18]

One way I experience Christmas as a spirituality is through the prayer of that most enthusiastic convert, Ebenezer Scrooge: "Assure me that I yet may change these shadows you have shown me, by an altered life... I will honor Christmas in my heart, and try to keep it all the year. I will live in the past, the present, and the future. The Spirits of all Three shall strive within me. I will not shut out the lessons that they teach."[19] God bless us, every one.

And what of my own creativity? "Generative care," the Whiteheads explain, "is able to let go, to release without bitterness, that which has been generated. But this mature letting go applies not only to the works of our hands but to our very sense of self generated over the previous decades. Persons are more than what they do, more than the sum of what they have become." The Whiteheads say that for many adults this is a fleeting insight. For me it is becoming dominant.

We are more than our accomplishments! We are more than our achievements. God does not love us because of what we have done but because of who we are. Our transformation, our growth in grace, is a growth that comes from yielding, from acceptance. The lilies of the field do not toil and do not spin.

One thing I notice in my mother, my husband, and myself. We are more willing, perhaps, to be children than ever before. Bill has always had a fey imagination. Now he is willing to give way to his impulse to write stories about rabbits nesting in stained-glass church windows, ear to ear: fables (with ecological themes) about the creatures who live around the lagoon in New Orleans' Audubon Park. For myself I am drawn by love of fairy tales and nursery rhymes in which I see mystical meanings I never understood in earlier times of my life. Possibly the life-voyage is really on crystal seas of spiritual imagination.

> Wynken, Blynken and Nod one night
> Sailed off in a wooden shoe
> Sailed on a river of crystal light
> Into a sea of dew.
> Where are you going, and what do you wish,
> The old moon asked the three.
> We have come to fish for the flying fish
> That live in this beautiful sea,
> Said Wynken, Blynken and Nod.

CHAPTER EIGHT

Wings of Morning

IN A SUNDAY MAGAZINE I FIND A CONTROVERSY raging about beauty and old age. The newspaper has published a fashion feature of six women who "look wonderful for their age." A reader writes to challenge them. What, she wants to know, was the point of it? "Was it to illustrate that beautiful women age beautifully? And what are the perceptions of 'age and beauty' that she says are being changed here? There are none that I can see. She says the six women pictured look wonderful for their age. In fact, they don't look their age at all. What is wrong with looking forty or fifty or sixty? In a society that has dozens of negative words for aging women and precious few positive ones, the message of articles like this is clear: deny the process as long as possible."[1]

Is old age beautiful? Often it is angelic! Reflecting on this, I travel on wings of the mind back to a brisk October morning in the late 1950s. The place is a southern college for women, Sophie Newcomb College of Tulane University. It is a small campus of low brick structures linked by arches, shaded by oaks, clumped with palmettoes. Morning chapel is still regularly observed in accordance with Mrs. Newcomb's will.

Picture a senior, flapping along in academic gown to lead prayers and Scripture readings to a sparse assembly of souls. Picture me, a confused and bookish sophomore, loving the solemnity of chapel but not knowing what to believe about God.

The bell rings. Students mill about in the hallway. Their chatter is about dates, dances, sorority meetings, bridge games. Why do I want to be like the others but feel I can't be? Why do I see every experience from the outside, observe every incident as if to write about it? Why do I want so much to fathom the universe, to decipher the riddle of things?

In that solitary space defined by intellect and poetic dreaming, I drift into Sophomore English, there to fall under the spell of a small, white-haired professor of English literature. Dr. Mildred Gayler Christian was for me, as for many other students, something of what Vergil was to Dante, a guide to far reaches of mind and heart.

Now I can hardly imagine the Communion of Saints without thinking of her. It was her commanding presence that brought a flood of light into my nineteenth year. Though I was one of forty sophomores enrolled in her second-year English Lit class, my exchange with her began with dialogue. I had written a paper on Matthew Arnold's sonnet about Shakespeare, mentioning the confusing statement in line eleven, and the phrase, "Better so!" In the margin of that paper, Christian penciled this elaborate response:

The final paragraph expresses exactly what I feel about the phrasing. I remain baffled, no matter how often and how carefully I read this sonnet. On the whole, I have concluded that Arnold means to say that again and again we question the nature of genius, baffled by it and seeking to understand it. But it, without superciliousness, recognizes its own superiority and our inability to comprehend it in full. So it leaves only so much of itself exposed as we may approximately understand (through its work); and *that* tells us that it has spoken for man's sorrows [*sic*] with such profound completeness that we are content to let genius speak for us. 'Better so!' (Others—men lesser than Shakespeare—submit to our questions, even by implication, try to answer us. But only a lesser talent *will* try; genius in its wisdom is silent in recognition of our inability to master the answer, were one given.)

That penciled note is a fragmentary reminder of the blessing of those days. My love of English poetry and prose was already a fiery experience of revelation. Mildred Christian heaped coals—or were they diamonds?—on that fire.

TEACHER AND ANGEL

"For in him we live, and move, and have our being."[2] From the first moments of our acquaintance, Mildred Christian and I were somehow at one. Her face, voice (speaking or singing), handwriting, knowledge of English writers and criticism, clear vision of reality, example of faith, all these became suddenly dear to me. Mind you, I could not yet have called it friendship. Miss Christian was of the old school, and held herself aloof from students. What I felt was neither cozy nor intimate, but an invitation to enter a vast universe. A new, shared way of seeing things crashed through my walls of isolation; everything seemed lighted up from within.

Dozens of women who were her students recall this same intensity, this sense of meaning through poetry that Mildred Christian gave them. "Oh, did you have Miss Christian?" "Do you remember her in Milton class?" "I loved the way she taught the Brontës." Each of us remembers, and the circle that binds us has a heavenly parallel. Theologically, I can now state the reason which then eluded me. This was a friendship forged in Jesus Christ.

Did I know I was beginning one of the most formative relationships in my life? Hardly. In a random, haphazard way I was dealing with an interior struggle: trying to integrate the experiences of youth with those of literature, including the Bible. In courses meant for instruction in English, I wrestled to frame theological questions. I was fascinated with seventeenth-century writers and wanted to know if modern people could believe as they did. Could anyone now take George Herbert, John Donne, and John Milton seriously? Even with nineteenth-century writers, I knew what a chasm yawned between them and us.

I did not see that while I was studying poetry, what I was learning was Christianity. C.S. Lewis describes a similar experience in his story of conversion, *Surprised by Joy: The Shape of My Early Life.* All the while he was resisting the possibility of faith, he found that his favorite writers were believers. While he thought himself an agnostic, he should have been drawn, by all rights, to the agnostics and atheists, but found their work hollow and unsatisfying. Christian writers attracted him, on the other hand, for everything *except* their Christianity.

My situation was not perhaps so clear-cut. I was not actively fleeing from faith. But when I met Milton, for example, I felt surrounded by hierarchies of heavenly beings, awed by Satan's murky legions, caught by the sweep and splendor of Milton's long and resonant blank-verse line. I marveled at the way he could move the narrative ahead, while studding his verses with mythological beings—all this was an experience of heaven, bliss from which a nineteen-year-old's heart hardly cared to return.

Mildred Christian was, surely, the angel of the Miltonic gate; behind me it clanged shut, and I was summoned into that space of intellect, intuition, and imagination from which I would never want to be free again.

A C.S. LEWIS CONNECTION

Now there is a lapse of some twenty years. Now, living in New York City, I have become wiser in worldly matters, have experienced losses and reversals, learned some of my breaking points. Prayer has become my lifeline to sanity. Now the writings of those earlier faith-filled centuries, especially those of John Donne and John Milton, make sense. I'm still struggling to realize my life's ambition of becoming a writer. I am writing *Turning*, a book about religious conversion. One evening, after a meeting of the C.S. Lewis Society in Manhattan, I decide to write to Mildred Christian.

I wrote, thanking her for her influence on my life and especially my acceptance of Christianity. She replied:

Your beautiful letter leaves me feeling very humble. I feel that you credit me with more than I deserve, but I am deeply touched that you believe me a force for good in your life. Thank you profoundly. Your letter arrived on a day when I was down-hearted—and cured me at once, especially as its contents were so unexpected! I want you to know that, while you wait for my letter—to follow. [She had promised me a second letter.] Meanwhile, renew acquaintance with George Herbert. He seems to me a natural fourth to your triumvirate." [I had mentioned three writers who influenced me.]

FRIENDSHIP DEEPENS IN LATER LIFE

So the friendship was taken up again, focusing on mutual interests: C.S. Lewis, my new book, *Turning*, her lifelong research on Charlotte Brontë. At once I was asked to drop around to Christie's in New York where a group of Brontë letters were being offered for sale. Visits to New Orleans followed. I was gradually briefed on her two projected works on the Brontës.

Later that year my husband and I decided to move to New Orleans. The three of us lunched together, and joyful as it was, I felt a sorrow that I could not drop everything and become Miss Christian's scholarly disciple. Her Brontë project, I felt, would not be completed without some substantial editorial and scholarly help. Yet she went relentlessly on, rehearsing the story with me of snags that kept her from publication, and, on her last visit to the Brontë parsonage in Haworth, continuing to keep me informed on the progress of her work.

In an effort to encourage my Christian writing, she gave me a copy of Charles Colson's *Loving God*. I think the sentiments suited her, although the writing style did not. When *Clinging*, my book on prayer, was published, Miss Christian wrote me from The Brontë Parsonage, Haworth, on September 2, 1984:

Emilie, this book is superior to your first. It is better expressed, is more condensed, has a delightful (and shrewd) sense of humor in sections, is beautifully honest and, I believe, indeed serves God in providing some record of your own meditations and experiences in prayer. It invites to meditation by others, without prescribing a "method." Good! I feel blessed to have had even a very remote part in it, in introducing you to George Herbert. Would that all my students had been as perceptive as you of the power and beauty of the poetry of the seventeenth century! I rejoice in you, dear, and thank you for your accomplishment.

Again on October 28 of the same year she wrote from The Brontë Parsonage to acknowledge a reminiscence I had written for a Tulane University magazine.

My reward comes in recognizing the uses you have made of your learning, dedicated to the search to know the nature of

God and expressing your worship of him in terms marked by sincerity and certainty. Conviction breathes through everything you say. I am deeply satisfied that you have indeed found the way "to the heart and center of things"—*your* phrase. Thank you for sharing your discoveries with me.

Did any student ever have such a reward for her efforts? More and more, as I came to know her better, I saw her in the light of George Herbert. The reason was her modesty and humility. She was conscious of her unworthiness and expressed it simply.

Your beautiful letter reached me on a day when I felt such a keen disappointment in the state of my own Christianity that your generously crediting me with a beneficent influence on your spiritual life came as a balm to my spirit. (June 26, 1979)

That was so like Herbert's poem, I thought:

Love bade me welcome: yet my soul drew back,
    Guilty of dust and sin.
But quickey'd love, observing me grow slack
    From my first entrance in,
Drew nearer to me, sweetly questioning,
    If I lack'd anything.[3]

A FORETASTE OF HEAVEN

Miss Christian also showed a mystic's gift for experiencing beauty in the simplest things, such as her own New Orleans garden after a rainstorm:

It is now the 14th and New Orleans has experienced such a downpour as I cannot recall having ever heard or watched.

During it, hail fell now and again. The azaleas were sodden at the height of their bloom; so were the amaryllis blooms, and the sprays of bridal wreath. The roses showered down, and the trees rained leaves in such numbers that one expected to see bare branches above him. Not so; the magnolias shine in their fresh cleansing.

There are many moments in our friendship I might remember as glimpses of heaven. Perhaps the tenderest is Mardi Gras Day, 1985. By then Miss Christian had given up her New Orleans house and had gone to live at St. Anna's residence, not far from the main parade route. The streets were filled with maskers and revelers. Together we walked two blocks to stand in the chill wind and wait for the parade of Rex, king of this unruly festival, to pass by. A young man suddenly approached us with a bunch of long-stemmed yellow chrysanthemums and pressed them into Miss Christian's hands. I understood his sudden affectionate impulse. Miss Christian's shining face was an invitation to friendship. Later, after leaving her, I walked on the grounds of my high school, meditating on how God had constantly broken through to me through books, through teachers, through poetry. From the upstairs balcony of the school, I had a partial view of the parade, and one word, only one, on the side of a passing truck float, stayed in view for a long moment. The word was HEAVEN.

"I want this copy of George Herbert to come to you eventually," she had told me in 1980, putting the heavy and somewhat intimidating volume (Oxford: 1941) into my hands and expecting me to make good use of it. After her death, through the good graces of Tulane and her relations, the book did come to me. As I leaf over the pages and read the sharp, scholarly marginal comments, I know that I am loved, and how abundantly.

In *Clinging* I said that spiritual friendships are forged on the anvil of grace. There I also described the way such friendships become intensified after one of the partners dies: "The friendship is strengthened and purified, it seems, by this death, which we say is not cessation but passage into deeper perception of God. The presence of that person becomes more so in the lives of those left behind. It is as though the blinding intensity of heaven were being shared, over the boundary, and the life of God were flowing more readily into us through them."[4]

THE STRENGTH OF LOVE

At the close of her life she was afflicted with failing memory, confusion, disorientation, the inability to complete her scholarly work. It was heartbreaking to see this decline. On the day that she was honored for her contributions to Newcomb College in 1986, my mother and I, both former students of hers, went to St. Anna's to escort her to the ceremony on campus. I brought a card with me on which was printed Shakespeare's sonnet, "To me, fair friend, you never can be old." She did not appear to recognize it. The decline continued, sharply, until her death in 1989. There was no remedy, no answer, but faith. Because of this sorrow I like to remember one of her favorite lines, from Wordsworth's *Michael:*

There is a comfort in the strength of love
'Twill make endurable, a thing which else
Would overturn the brain or break the heart.[5]

Overtaken by a flood of tears in the library of Trinity Church (where Miss Christian and I had attended a tea after the Lewis lecture), I opened the *Book of Common Prayer* and found these words:

Almighty God, the fountain of all wisdom: enlighten by your Holy Spirit those who teach and those who learn, that, rejoicing in the knowledge of your truth, they may worship you and serve you from generation to generation; through Jesus Christ Our Lord, who lives and reigns with you and the Holy Spirit, One God, forever and ever. Amen.

Miss Christian was one of those who taught me to trust the glimpses of God found in experience, to pass through prison walls with poetic insight. She knew that poetry and Scripture offer bread for the journey. Even in her apparent loss of sovereignty I could see the imprint of God's design. Such, for us all, is the freedom of the believer who trusts in the necessity and nobility of the life process.

CHAPTER NINE

Souls in
Full Sail

I N A VERY SHORT AND VERY WISE BOOK on the spiritual life, called *Abandonment to Divine Providence* by Jean-Pierre de Causadde, I find these riveting words: "The present moment always reveals the presence and the power of God. Every moment we live through is like an ambassador who declares the will of God, and our hearts always utter their acceptance."[1] Well, our hearts do voice acceptance, but perhaps not *always*, but in due course. "Our souls steadily advance, never halting, but sweeping along with every wind." (I must conclude that my soul is in full sail. The sixteenth-century journey of exploration is the same as my own.) "Every current," writes de Caussade, the author of this small treatise, "every technique thrusts us onward in our voyage to the infinite." De Caussade, my brother of the heart, and I are on the same voyage. Centuries apart, we are both setting our course for the heart of Christ.

I understand now how I have wanted to set out on some expedition, attempt some major discovery, some giant uncharted journey *for the sake of the kingdom.* Or was it only for my own sake, to see my name in lights? For the sake of my legacy, my posterity, my immortality. Now I appreciate John Milton in his old age, blind, and suffering from gout, demanding of those unwilling daughters that they take his dictation of two major English epics. It was, no doubt, God's work, if not a very kind thing to do.

Even more than Milton, I think Dante is my kinsman. Hasn't each one of us saved some precious enterprise for the last? All three books of *The Divine Comedy* yawn before me. (Shall I try to read them in Italian, as Dorothy Sayers did, and try my own translation? Or shall I learn to love the lilt and fall of *terza rima*, untranslated? Is there time to learn Italian and Greek and Anglo-Saxon and Hebrew in the years that remain? The epic languages, one might say?)

Throughout *The Divine Comedy* the metaphor of the ship describes the pilgrim's journey and the movement of the poem. Dante sets his course for an uncharted sea, and travels through the realms of hell, purgatory, and paradise. He sees himself as a new Jason, who journeys to find the golden fleece. This fleece of his is the vision of God. In a full poetic vision Dante has captured the spiritual journey.

I have tried before to read the poem, starting with the first book on hell. I have always lost interest after awhile and set it aside. This time I resolve to skip over to the third book, on paradise, in spite of John Freccero's statement, in his preface to Ciardi's *Paradiso* translation, that most modern people can't identify with it. "Few of us still believe in paradise in any form," Freccero insists, but he says that the daring of the poem is still worthwhile, even contemporary.[2]

But I don't see the world the way John Freccero does. To me, however "medieval" the context, there are a few things that make *The Paradiso* a joy to read. For one thing, I do believe in paradise. But what I believe about it is contemporary, not medieval.

This love does not exist in any place
But in God's mind, where burns the love that turns it
And the power that rains to it from all of space.[3]

Each poet takes the cosmic scenario dealt to him by his own generation and sees God's love burning at the center, the ground of all being, the power that drives the planets and the stars, that also makes its home in our hearts.

Quite right, too, to see the vision of God revealed by mystical and erotic love! Everything in this cosmic vision of his seems to make sense in terms of our experience of love and the hope of human transformation which is no medieval trope, but as fresh and as possible now as it ever was.

SALVATION THROUGH LOVE

In remembering the people in my life who have gone before me, people of simplicity and faith, I am childlike enough to embrace biblical metaphors. In this poem I wrote about the death of my grandmother, called "Remembering Lucy Powell Russell," I wanted to do that. I hope also (though it is inconceivable to me) for the grace to enter into the metaphor of my own death.

When we went through her clothes
and her jewelry-box
I thought how she loved pretty things.

And I remembered
she wouldn't need them in heaven.
Everything lovely is already there.

The gowns of the blessed
are more dazzling

than anything we'd stitch together.
Anyone who loved looking pretty, as she did
ought to be happy there.
There are no tears.
There are no tatters.
There is no sorrow or pining.
And the light of his countenance shining round
glorifies all who are there.

Doesn't it say in the Bible somewhere
that he will give us
wedding-garments to wear?

"A thought transfixed me," wrote Viktor Frankl in his reflection on concentration camp experience, "for the first time in my life I saw the truth as it is set into song by so many poets, proclaimed as the final wisdom by so many thinkers. The truth—that love is the ultimate and highest goal to which man can aspire. Then I grasped the meaning of the greatest secret that human poetry and human thought and belief have to impart: *The salvation of man is through love and in love...* For the first time in my life I was able to understand the meaning of the words, 'the angels are lost in perpetual adoration of an infinite glory.'"[4]

MODELS OF FIDELITY

Certain writers are models for me of a life well-lived. Some have lived lives shorter than mine, but they have lived so well. I think of Dorothy L. Sayers, who died in 1957, at sixty. When she was my age she was already affecting a monocle; she had become the elder stateswoman of Christianity and the arts. Catherine Marshall, the Presbyterian spiritual writer whose life influenced me, died before reaching the full bloom of old age. Yet her books on the Holy Spirit, on the experience of Christian marriage and widowhood, and her novels sold in the megamillions and touched countless lives. I am conscious that William Shakespeare lived only into his fifties, and I revere his life achievement, his capacity for joy.

What is the common thread among these figures I admire? Perhaps it is the capacity to transcend the limits of one's own life by fidelity to a task, the capacity to live well. Another figure who engages me is Gerard Manley Hopkins, who became a major poet in spite of his times, in spite of rejections, in spite of hardship and misunderstanding.

It is a short life and bears re-telling. Hopkins was born in Stratford, Essex, in 1844, the eldest son in a literary and artistic family. His parents were devout Anglicans. He attended Highgate School, where he showed great literary promise and won a prize for his first surviving poem, "The Escorial."

In 1863, at nineteen, he went to Balliol College, Oxford. In the same year he published "Winter with the Gulf Stream." At Oxford he made many friends, including Robert Bridges, and wrote a great deal of poetry, including "Heaven-Haven" and "The Habit of Perfection." He obtained a First Class degree. During his college years he came under the influence of the Oxford Movement and John Henry Newman, and he was received into the Roman Catholic Church (1866).

In 1868 he decided to become a Jesuit. He symbolically burned his poems but sent them at the same time to Bridges for safekeeping. For the next few years he wrote little, devoting himself to the life of a novice at Roehampton and to study at Stonyhurst; he was professor of rhetoric at Roehampton, then studied theology at St. Beuno's in North Wales where he also learned Welsh. During this period he was developing his theories of "instress," "inscape," and "sprung rhythm."

A new phase of creativity began in 1876. Inspired by the loss of the passenger ship *Deutschland* in December 1875, which had among its passengers five Franciscan nuns exiled for their faith, Hopkins, encouraged by his rector, wrote his most ambitious poem, "Wreck of the Deutschland." It was rejected by the Jesuit journal, *The Month*, as too difficult for its readers, but Hopkins, strengthened by his spiritual directors, continued to write, and in 1877, while studying for ordination, wrote some of his best-known poems, including "The Windhover" and "Pied Beauty." After ordination he was sent to Chesterfield, then London, then Oxford. He worked in various industrial parishes, including an exhausting spell in Liverpool where he was deeply depressed by a sense of his failure as a preacher.

In 1881 R.W. Dixon, an admiring former teacher from his Highgate years, persuaded Hopkins to submit some sonnets to an anthology. These were also rejected. Dixon tried to persuade Hopkins, without success, to set aside his view that he should publish only if encouraged by his superiors. Hopkins worked briefly in Glasgow, returned again to Roehampton and Stonyhurst, then in 1884 was appointed to the chair of Greek and Latin at University College, Dublin. There he found himself overcome with administrative and academic work, became ill and depressed, and wrote his "Dark Sonnets" (1885) expressing a sense of exile and frustration ("Carrion Comfort" and "No worst, there is none"). He wrote to Bridges expressing weakness and desolation, but in his last years wrote more hopeful poems. Among these "That Nature is a Heraclitean Fire" and "Thou art indeed just, Lord" (March 1889). He died in June of typhoid.

Hopkins' poetry was not published until 1918. Now he is recognized as a major poet. His poems, letters, and journals show the breadth of his vision: his sense of vocation as priest and poet; his appreciation of beauty in man and nature; technical theoretical work in prosody; longing for a unifying view of experience. Hopkins coined the terms "inscape" (the individual or essential quality of a thing) and "instress" (the energy which sustains an inscape). His term, "sprung rhythm," Hopkins meant as a harking back to earlier rhythms of speech and forms of verse once common in England.

In Margaret Drabble's essay about Hopkins in the *Oxford Companion to English Literature* she suggests that Hopkins' originality lies not in his technical innovations but rather in his fresh poetic drive and energy after a period of derivative poetry in the later nineteenth century. Recently a contemporary American writer, Dan Wakefield, with whom I was visiting at a conference on religion and the arts held in Berkeley, said that he thought Hopkins a very important poet, striking and adventurous in his use of language.

This courageous use of English, this willingness to turn handsprings with words and metaphors, is matched by Hopkins' passionate willingness to take chances with life. Hopkins risked everything for God. His passionate commitment to Jesus Christ in the Church cost him a great deal; and at the same time I think this tremendous gamble, this risking everything for God, and his willingness to embrace Jesuit obedience (however it tethered and constrained him) is what set Hopkins free for an almost childlike gamboling on the hillsides. This restrictiveness of the Jesuit life, combined with the mystical intensity of his rule-bound spirituality, gave rise to a special kind of focus. Hopkins was able to structure the whole of creation into world-embracing metaphors, crystalline images that reveal cosmic realities.

A second figure of large influence also must come into the story: John Henry Newman. The most significant image we must pluck from Newman's vast and influential life-canvas is simply that of the one who risks all for Jesus Christ. Newman loved the Church of England as deeply as anyone has; but ultimately, it seemed to him that this love of Anglicanism must be placed on the altar, offered up as fragrant incense to the Lord. This experience was costly for Newman. It was deeply painful. It required him to leave Oxford, his natural earthly and scholarly home; to leave the beauty and loveliness of the Church of England, with all the allegiances it stood for; and to squeeze into the narrow space of a church which was in its externals ugly, dank, pompous, and foreign, reeking of Irish poverty and Italian affectation.

This chance which Newman took with his life at forty-four is reminiscent to me of Thomas More's decision to go to the gallows instead of passing free through the prison door. An intellectual compromise for either man would have resulted in a long and comfortable life, filled with appropriate external consolations. But More and Newman were driven from within by the demands of a visionary understanding and a relentless conscience. I say this without even mentioning the possibility of grace.

This passage which Newman made was not his first, but a further conversion experience. At fifteen he had experienced the joy of an evangelical-style conversion, though Newman could never have been called an Evangelical in the strict sense. But that youthful energy of giving his life to Christ in his early days was part of the constantly renewed and renewing religious drive that made this man such a remarkable and influential Christian.

In the years that Newman withdrew to Littlemore, not far from Oxford, he attempted to build a spiritual retreat, adopting a semi-monastic way of life. An observer said of this place:

It was said in those days that the approach to Oxford by the Henley road was the most beautiful in the world. Soon after passing Littlemore you came in sight of, and did not lose again, that sweet city with its dreaming spires, driven along a road now crowded and obscured with dwellings, open then to the cornfields on the right, to undisclosed meadows on the left, with an unbroken view of the long line of towers, rising out of foliage.... At once, without suburban interval, you entered the finest quarter of the town, rolling under Magdalen Tower, and past the Magdalen elms, then in full unmutilated luxuriance, till the exquisite curves of the High Street opened on you, as you drew up at The Angel, or passed on to the Mitre and the Star.[5]

Eighteen years later, the young Hopkins, in his first year at Balliol, went out for an afternoon visit to Littlemore, and the two lives became connected. Listen to Hopkins writing home to his mother from Balliol College on 22 April 1863.[6]

My rooms are, I suppose you know, in the roof, which slopes up to the middle of the ceiling. Running up and down between lectures is exhausting. However from four of my six windows I have the best views in Balliol, and my staircase has the best scout in the college. My rooms are three, bedroom, sitting-room, and cellar. I have no scout's hole, and no oak to sport when necessary.

This is the program of my day—7:15, get up, dress; 8, chapel; 8:30, breakfast; 10, lecture; 11, second ditto; 12, sometimes third ditto; 1-2, buttery open for lunch; afternoon, boating or walking and following your own devices; 5, evening chapel, which I have never yet attended; 5:30, the hall; 6, the Union; 7 to bed-time, tea and preparing lectures....

Yesterday afternoon, Strachan-Davidson and I went boating on the upper river. We took a sailing boat, sculled up and sailed down. We then took canoes. I know nothing so luxuriously delicious as a canoe. It is a long light covered boat, the same shape both ways, with an opening in the middle where you recline, your feet against one board, your back against a cushion on another. You look, contrary of course to ordinary boats, in the direction in which you are going, and move with a single paddle—a rod with a broad round blade at either end which you dip alternately on either side. The motion is Elysian. Strahan-Davidson's canoe being very low in the water and the wind being very high and making waves, he shipped much water, till he said that it was more pleasant than safe, and had to get to shore and bale out the water, which had nearly sunk him. I, rejoicing in the security of a boat high in the water and given me because large and safe, was meanwhile washed onto the opposite lee shore where I was comfortable but embarrassed, and could not get off it for some time. Altogether it was Paradisiacal. A canoe in the Cherwell must be the summit of human happiness. On Saturday morning I breakfasted with Palmer, on Sunday Papa and I with Bond, on Tuesday I with Jowett. Jowett is my tutor; when you can get him to talk he is amusing, but when the opposite, it is terribly embarrassing.

This afternoon I walked with Addis [his friend William Addis] to Littlemore Church which Newman's mother built, and where was Newman's last sermon before the exodus. It is quite dark when you enter, but the eye soon becomes accustomed to it. Every window is of the richest stained glass; the east end, east window, altar and reredos are exquisite; the decorations being on a small scale, but most elaborate and perfect. It is a pity Margaret St. Church could not have borrowed something from it. I can not go on describing all Oxford, its inhabitants and its neighborhood, but to be short, everything is delightful, I have met with much attention and am perfectly comfortable....

Hopkins already was conscious of all the drama of Newman's conversion. So his casual little visit was perhaps not so casual. In my early religious pilgrimage I was also a frequenter of churches and other holy places. I remember how keen I was to see the actual spot where Thomas á Becket supposedly fell, in Canterbury Cathedral; and to see the place in the crypt where his remains were once honored by the Canterbury pilgrims. To be in the places where the great events of religious history occurred is to live them again, to gain the grace of them, somehow, in one's own life.

Hopkins remained close to his parents. In spite of the breach caused by his religious choices, the relationship healed and remained strong throughout his lifetime. Many of his letters indicate this, but none more so than his birthday letter to his mother written March 2, 1880 from 8 Salisbury Street, Liverpool:

My dearest Mother—I wish you many happy returns of tomorrow; by great good luck, for we seldom have the opportunity of applying the mass to our own intentions, I was able to say mass for you this morning.

Every time I look at the stole you made I think it handsomer: I blessed it... yesterday. I believe however I could satisfy you that they can be made lighter, for I have a lighter and more portable one: it is not, I think, of ribbon.

The stole she made him I take to be a sign of her acceptance of his priesthood. His reference to the restrictions on his intentions at Mass is a reminder to me of the church the way it was. We of the later twentieth century can hardly reconstruct the psychological and emotional constraints of Jesuit obedience in Hopkins' time.

In the same letter he speaks of his ongoing contact with Newman:

I wrote, as I do every year, to Cardinal Newman on his birthday the 31st of last month. I got by return of post a pretty little card of a spray of dogwood leaves, one green, two red and withered, symbolical perhaps of age, run through a card or piece of paper on which was written, "Many, many thanks. Pardon so brief an answer. J.H.N." with a date.

Newman's correspondence was vast. He was by now quite along in years. While Hopkins' life was short, Newman's was very long. To him, Hopkins was perhaps only one of many younger men who came under his influence. He could not have known the breadth of Hopkins' vision or the size of his talent.

The parallels between Newman and Hopkins have little to do with literature. Though both men were gifted writers, they existed in very different spheres and were moving on what now seem to be entirely different timetables. Each man was in his own way a giant. Yet as men of letters it seems to me their paths did not entirely cross; they did not understand each other.

On another plane, however, they are soul-brothers. When Hopkins joined the Society of Jesus, Newman solaced him in his doubts. "Don't call the Jesuit discipline hard," Newman said. "It will bring you to heaven."

When in 1887 Hopkins went to University College, Dublin, as professor, Newman confided in Hopkins that if he were an Irishman he would be in heart a rebel.

This was the stuff these men were made of: courageous, bold spirits surrendered to lives of fidelity and obedience. As converts both were painfully uncomfortable—misfits, unable entirely to accommodate to the new cultures in which they found themselves.

This painful obedience was the narrow path on which each one walked. Poetically and prayerfully, they poured out the pain in ways that we can profit from. These words, widely known as "Newman's prayer," express that:

God has created me to do him some definite service.
He has committed some work to me which he has not
    committed to another.
I have my mission.
I may never know it in this life
But I shall be told it in the next.
I am a link in a chain.
A bond of connection between persons
He has not created me for naught
I shall do good—I shall do his work
I shall be an angel of peace
A preacher of truth in my own place
While not intending it
If I do but keep his commandments.
Therefore I will trust him
Whatever I am, I can never be thrown away.

If I am in sickness, my sickness may serve him
In perplexity, my perplexity may serve him
If I am in sorrow, my sorrow may serve him
He does nothing in vain
He knows what he is about
He may take away my friends
He may throw me among strangers
He may make me feel desolate
Make my spirits sink
Hide my future from me—still
He knows what he is about.[7]

That deep sense of vocation and fidelity in the midst of darkness is Newman's; and it is Hopkins' gift as well:

As kingfishers catch fire, dragonflies draw flame;
As tumbled over rim in roundy wells
Stones ring; like each tucked string tells, each hung bell's
    Bow swung finds tongue to fling out broad its name;
Each mortal thing does one thing and the same;
Deals out that being indoors each one dwells;
Selves—goes itself; *myself* it speaks and spells,
Crying *What I do is me: for that I came.*

Fearful, lonely, desolate, depressed, Hopkins yet brings us a counsel of faith and hope:

I say móre: the just man justices
Keeps grace: thát keeps all his goings graces;
Acts in God's eye what in God's eye he is—
Chríst—for Christ plays in ten thousand places,
Lovely in limbs and lovely in eyes not his
To the Father through the features of men's faces.[8]

VICTORIAN EMINENCE

In his book, *Eminent Victorians*, A.N. Wilson says that Newman's conversion changed the religious complexion of England. I feel a sadness about Wilson. Clearly a man who has felt a fascination with religion from his earliest days, he seems nevertheless incapable of grasping the nettle of it as Newman and Hopkins were able to do. Yet I see that Wilson is the third, faltering member of this spiritual circle. Newman and Hopkins are stretching out their hands to him but he will not dance.

Passionately attracted to Newman in his youth, Wilson once read him obsessively. "The first thing I did when I arrived in Oxford as an undergraduate was to walk out to Littlemore."[8] Today, Wilson says, despite his religious longings, he can't enter into the believing mentality of the Victorians or construct one that works for his own age, our age.

Shortly after reading this rather familiar and predictable confession of Wilson's, I chanced upon these words of Newman's: "I have known the case of a person taking up religion for a time and seeming to be religious and then casting it off, and giving up even the belief in God... and confessing it, confessing it in language such as this: 'I was religious once. Religion had its day with me. It grew up, like the grass, and has come to nought like the grass. I can't revive it. It was a certain state of mind of a certain period of my life, but I have outgrown it.'"[10]

The effect of reading these words—laying them against Wilson's, as it were, in my imagination—was striking. What advice would Newman offer for this person drifting into apostasy?

Hebrews 3:7-8, 13, "Today if ye shall hear his voice, harden not your hearts, as in the provocation, according to the day of temptation in the wilderness... Exhort one another every day whilst it is called today, lest any be hardened by the deceitfulness of sin." The Victorian translation was antiquated, but the thoughts were crystal clear.

"And if you are conscious that your hearts are hard, and are desirous that they should be softened, do not despair. All things are possible to you, through God's grace."

And through Newman's voice, I heard Hopkins speaking:

O then, weary then whý should we tread? O why are we so
     haggard at the heart, so care-coiled, care-killed, so fagged,
     so fashed, so cogged, so cumbered,
When the thing we freely fórfeit is kept with fonder a care,
Fonder a care kept than we could have kept it, kept
Far with fonder a care (and we, we should have lost it)
     finer, fonder
A care kept.—Where kept? Do but tell us where kept,
     where.—
Yonder.—What high as that! We follow, now we follow.—
     Yonder, yes yonder, yonder,
Yonder.[11]

In this way Hopkins has contributed a new word, and a new idea, to my vocabulary: eastering. When Hopkins writes, in "Wreck of the Deutschland," that Christ should easter in us, I understand that he has turned a day in the Christian calendar into an ongoing work of grace. Hopkins stretches the word "to easter" beyond its plain nautical meaning of heading eastward. In Hopkins I come to understand that my wintering is eastering. Even the word grace is no longer a noun but a verb.

CHAPTER TEN

Eastering

"'I SHALL GET WELL! I shall get well!' he cried out. 'Mary! Dickon! I shall get well! And I shall live forever and ever and ever!'"

These stirring words, from the invalid boy Colin, in Frances Hodgson Burnett's novel, *The Secret Garden*, make a faith statement on many levels.

For me, eastering means becoming aware of the truth of the resurrection in sudden and surprising ways. And this somewhat Victorian children's book is about that. It is also about the influence of love in healing and recovery. The child-invalid, Colin, imprisoned by his own self-pity and willfulness, uses sickness as a way of maintaining center stage. His tantrums are pleas for attention; he is thinking his way into becoming a hunchback, like his self-pitying and neglectful father.

The story is melodramatic, and the screen version of it does not capture for me the sense of awe I once felt as a child, when, with the heroine Mary Lennox, I entered into dialogue with a robin and found the mysterious key that opened the neglected garden. Many years later, finding the book again, I opened it and found in it a metaphor of prayer. Prayer is the narrow door which we must unlock in order to find renewal in our lives. God's presence has been there all along. He is passionately waiting for us in the garden if we will only seek his company there.

IN THE GARDEN

Do you remember
when you were five,
that moment,
just before dark,
when the fireflies winked
and a beautiful peace
stole swiftly on,
and you thought,
let them not call me in just yet,
please,
it is so lovely here, just now.
And you thought,
I shall never have
this unbearable sweetness,
this joy,
ever again.
Do you remember?

Now that I am eight times five
my prayer is like that.
The Lord takes me
into a garden
just at twilight.
His presence is unbearably sweet.
And I pray,
please Lord,
let me stay,
just another moment, here.

And then, he answers me.
Mind you, I don't know quite how.
This, he says, is only a taste
of what will be,
later,
when you come to me
forever and ever.

It takes some faith
to believe in things like that
until they happen to you.
Then, you want to run out into the garden
again and again.

The Secret Garden seems a throwback to earlier Victorian writing. When Colin, Mary, and Dickon send a message to Colin's father to return to them in the garden, it is heard by him at a great distance and as if he heard his dead wife calling from the garden. This scene is reminiscent of Jane Eyre, hearing Mr. Rochester's call for help after the destruction of Thornfield; in Charlotte Brontë's story, Jane's call is heard by Rochester as well.

No doubt this is part of the Celtic gift of paranormal experience, heightened by strong poetic imagination. But this book takes seriously, as our Victorian ancestors did, the possibility that someone who has died is still alive and acting for good in our lives. Colin's dead mother speaks to him, not only from her portrait hidden behind curtains in his room, but also in the beauty of the garden she loved.

This same willingness to use the religious imagination is still available a century later. If we are willing to use it we can enter into a more childlike and refreshing relationship with God. If we suppress that imagination we are killing part of ourselves, part of our human giftedness. If we give way to it we are enriching our capacity to experience the heights and depths of spiritual life. At last we can take the wings of morning and easter in the farthest reaches of the sea.

SURPRISING PRAYER

There's one sort of prayer that I have to call prayer of surprises. It is a sudden and very concrete sense that God is present to me, something almost like childhood experiences of play. Someone's hands are over my eyes. I can't see him, but he's saying, "Here I am." I almost hate to mention it because I know it's completely out of left field. There's nothing I can plan for or anticipate. Even to name it might make it seem available, when in fact it's always entirely possible and at the same time completely out of reach.

A concrete example in my own life: me, on a Saturday afternoon, suddenly bolting from the house with my Bible in hand, fleeing from the ganged-up responsibilities of living. (I don't mean anything too unusual, really, just the layer upon layer of commonplace obligations and anxieties... no personal space... no time for God or for myself.) So then, I light in a place of repose: the front steps of the neighborhood library. Around me, there's a vast lawn with brownish green grass, everything still a bit mucky from the last hard rain, not much comfort in the landscape... but then, as I open my Bible, a sound comes out of nowhere. A piper! The notes are so unearthly, so unreal, I try at first to ignore them.

The intrusion is completely out of whack, not related to my prayer agenda, even remotely. What does this piper have to do with me?

I open my Bible to Hosea 11. "When Israel was a child I loved him, and I called my son out of Egypt. But the more I called to them, the further they went from me; they have offered sacrifices to the Baals and set their offerings smoking before the idols."[1] Somehow the piper steals into my prayer, a haunting sound that's hard to ignore. Does the Piper stand for something with special meaning for me? "I myself taught Ephraim to walk, I took them in my arms," the Scripture continues.[2] I know it's a childhood metaphor, but what is the Lord trying to say? I feel the music bearing down on me, the sound and Scripture converge in my thoughts. Now I make a new association: the Pied Piper, leading the children (I'm one of them) out of Hamlin town. What a radical figure he cuts, there in his ragged garment with the odd assortment of colors. How much he reminds me that the Gospel power is something the people of the status quo fail to recognize. The Lord is speaking in riddles that make perfect sense to children but which adults fail to understand. He's spellbinding to those with open hearts.

"I led them with reins of kindness, with leading-strings of love. I was like someone who lifts an infant close against his cheek; stooping down to him I gave him his food."[3]

And is this same Piper here now in my prayer, speaking to me? "Because they have refused to return to me, the sword will rage through their towns, wiping out their children, glutting itself inside their fortresses."[4]

In the Scripture, as in the folktale, the stakes are very high. The Piper is playing for keeps. He expects nothing less than a full commitment, an honorable bargain, followed through to the last. And am I willing to walk with him? Into the mountainside? Taking the chance that the great side of the mountain will close up, and the children will never return?

The most important part of this surprising kind of prayer is catching the thread and following it even if the way lies into rough places and through the wilderness. The prayer of surprises is what happens when we are open, not only to the metaphors we decide on, but the ones that are flung in our path, impossible to avoid, challenging us, turning us in new directions. "Ephraim, how could I part with you? Israel, how could I give you up? How could I treat you like Admah, or deal with you like Zeboiim?"[5] It is hard to trust this Lord who is so demanding. Yet if we trust Scripture we have to take him at his word: "My whole being trembles at the thought. I will not give rein to my fierce anger, I will not destroy Ephraim again, for I am God, not man: I am the Holy One in your midst and have no wish to destroy."[6]

Finally I turn and steal a look at my real piper on the steps of the library. Sure enough, there is a person in worn jeans and jacket, a cap pulled down over his ears, piping a tune (It's actually "Oh the Days of the Kerry Dancers" but I'm definitely not in Ireland) and he looks more like a street-person than a leprechaun. At least I know the Piper is not entirely my own invention. The surprise, though, is finding him there, just at that time of special openness for me. I'm tempted to laugh out loud, it's so improbable. At the same time the guessing game is utterly serious. I feel the Lord wants to shake me out of my complacency. I sense the moment as a challenge, almost a reproach: "What description, then, can I find for the men of this generation? What are they like? They are like children shouting to one another while they sit in the marketplace: 'We played the pipes for you and you wouldn't dance; we sang dirges, and you wouldn't cry.'"[2]

The light is failing, but the Piper continues to play, and the Lord's voice is strong for me in his music. "The mysteries of the kingdom of God are revealed to you; for the rest there are only parables, so that they may see but not perceive, listen but not understand."[8] There are safer prayers, I suppose. There are formulas, things to recite, prayers to go to sleep by. But instead, because the world is in flames, and people of high courage are really needed, I can choose the prayer that opens me up to God's demands. "And some seed fell into rich soil and grew and produced its crop a hundredfold. Saying this he cried, 'Listen, anyone who has ears to hear!'"[9]

In the prayer of surprises I am a child, setting out with a high heart, to find a kingdom of peace and justice where they will do no war any more.

DOROTHY DAY AS GARDENER

"How can there be no God when there are all these beautiful things?" When the crepe myrtles are at their most intense, when the caladiums are brimming with raindrops, these words of Dorothy Day come to mind.

Planting, we stick our spades into the soil. We spot the birds nesting under the eaves. We smell how the rain releases some inner fragrance from the earth. There is beauty in things made by people, too. Even in them, as in natural things, we can see the beauty of God. Reason is beside the point. It's the things we love, and the people we love, that are our proofs for the existence of God.

But when I pray with Dorothy I am called to find beauty in unbeautiful places: where people are hopeless and in need. Poverty—spiritual and material—is her way into God's treasure. Can I follow where she leads? From my middle-class perch, can I enter into her Lower East Side circumstances, can I share her vantage point at least for a little while?

Leafing through a biographical treatment of Dorothy's life, Jim Forest's *Love Is the Measure*,[5] is almost like looking through a family album. In some ways it's hard to identify with that kind, worn face, the white hair and the wispy braids, possibly because I know I will never do such radical and radicalizing things, however much I might want to change this bad old world. I identify more easily with the young Dorothy, sitting on the beach at Staten Island with the man she loves. I appreciate the way she experienced God in her pregnancy; for her, having a baby was a metaphor of promise and peace. I know that woman. Also, childbirth was one of her most important learning experiences, which was also true for me. I am moved by the way she turned from unbelief and immorality... the way an abortion made her dream of motherhood! All this is concrete. And near to me. I can grasp it.

But to go to prison for the Lord's sake? Fearful to the last, my childhood ways come back. I was the one who sat on the grass while others climbed the tree. But even under the tree, God finds me. He is speaking through butterflies, the clover, the grass. His words are quiet, unmistakable. "Follow me, and I will make you a fisher of hearts..." I am called to love, to live, to work, to love God in and through my work. My call is not Dorothy's but my own. The Lord asks something difficult in this very moment. I must live the call of my time, my generation, my city, my poverty, my circumstance.

Myrtle is the poor person who comes to our door every week or so. Myrtle has just a few teeth but her spirit is wonderful. Then there's a fretful woman who stops me in the church door upset about the new parish liturgy. Is she also part of my call to the poor? Then there are the people who are trapped at the edge of employability, people who are hungry for opportunities they can't have; people who are hopelessly involved with drugs and alcohol. Are they my vulnerable poor? What about those who are spiritually starved, who hunger and thirst for something to believe in?

"People even brought little children to him, for him to touch them; but when the disciples saw this they turned them away. But Jesus called the children to him and said, 'Let the little children come to me, and do not stop them; for it is to such as these that the kingdom of God belongs.'"[11]

Following Dorothy, I pass through a narrow door, and the world I have entered is more real than the one I left behind. My companions on the road are a strange lot, and we know the way is dangerous. There are trials ahead. But we are willing pilgrims. We know that to enter in, we must pass through a reversal, a paradox. The hard path is also strewn with roses. Dorothy is leading me in the way of simplicity. It is the Lord's way. Love, as Dorothy tells us, is the measure by which we will be judged.

Suddenly I am sure I don't want to be the good-for-nothing servant, the one who simply stashed his talents and never tried to make them more. I don't want the great door to close against me. I want to follow the Lord, no matter how stony the path, how dangerous the way. "Happy are you when people abuse you and persecute you and speak all kinds of calumny against you on my account. Rejoice and be glad, for your reward will be great in heaven; this is how they persecuted the prophets before you."[12] Yet I know that melodrama is not the real stuff of spiritual life. Great tasks are those which crop up in front of us, the things given by circumstance as calls which we can't walk away from. We don't have to run after glamorous spiritual goals.

My reflection time is interrupted by the doorbell. It is Myrtle, and she has blessings to share: brand new teeth! I can't help thinking it's a sign of God's love for his faithful poor.

LEARNING TO SEE AGAIN

In a chapter called "The Birth of Vision," in his book *The Management of Time*, James T. McKay expands our understanding of what it is to see. First he mentions the situation of an eighteen-year-old man in the Mayo Clinic who has just undergone an operation to restore his sight. He asks us, and others, to imagine what the young man will see when the bandages are removed for the first time.

To give us insight into the experience, McKay quotes J.Z. Young, an authority on brain function: "The patient on opening his eyes gets little or no enjoyment; indeed, he finds the experience painful. He reports only a spinning mass of lights and colors. He proves to be quite unable to pick out objects by sight, to recognize what they are, or to name them. He has no conception of space with objects in it, although he knows all about objects and their names by touch. 'Of course,' you will say, 'he must take a little time to learn to recognize them by sight.' Not a *little* time, but a very long time, in fact, years. His brain *has not been trained in the rules of seeing.* We are not conscious that there are any such rules; we think we see, as we say, naturally. But we have in fact learned a whole set of rules during childhood."[13]

It seems that the very obvious spiritual changes of the life-voyage are our preparation to see something beyond our immediate sphere, something that we can only guess at and which will only later be revealed. It is not only wishful thinking that makes us say our lives are going somewhere. Even without the eyes of faith we sense a progression, a movement toward something. With the faith dimension it becomes almost a certainty.

I say almost a certainty because my own faith is in a God who will always leave something to our imagination, a sea that must be crossed by faith. *Then* we shall know as we can't presently know. The fullness of knowing can be sensed, can be dreamed of, can be anticipated, can be known by trust. But there is no way to get ahead of the story.

These are the principles of creative seeing that McKay outlines: 1. You are the creator of your own unique elements of experience, therefore you can change them at will. 2. You select and arrange the parts of your sensory impressions on the basis of your past experience. 3. As your experience in any area grows, you can see more in that area (make clearer, bigger, and more accurate mental pictures of what's going on). 4. Since your experience is never complete, you can never perceive *all* of what's going on; you always leave out a good deal in your observations.

The mind is its own place.[14] Always, our thought and our sense of ultimacy shapes what we feel, what we imagine, what we see. The winter voyage gives us the chance to anticipate a fuller, a deeper way of seeing. We must relent, release, surrender, in anticipation of another kind of knowing, far more exquisite than the breakthrough of first learning to read.

LIVING AT PINPOINTS

One advantage of living to be eighty-eight, according to Armand Hammer, is that, when you keep your wits about you, "the focus of your interests becomes pinpoint-precise." Hammer, in his autobiography, *Hammer*, recounts among other adventures his efforts toward world peace and a cure for cancer during the year from November 1984 to December 1985. Something about the grand scope of his ambitions (how many of us would dare hope to put a personal stamp on such solutions?) is almost funny. Nevertheless his sincerity is unquestionable, even if one hopes that Hammer is not just a Peter Sellers' Pink Panther character whose amateur efforts could make world diplomacy and scientific exploration worse.

"It is possible to see with absolute clarity what matters and what is unimportant," Hammer confides. "I know what I want to achieve in the time remaining to me, and if my ambitions are larger than many people's, that just means I have to try harder. I can't think of anything better to do with a life than to wear it out in efforts to be useful to the world."[15]

Hammer's dream and his energy are admirable. Surely, if persons at his level of power and prestige were consistently willing to put their efforts into such global aspirations, something good would be the result. The danger, of course, in such high aspirations, is to be tempted to earn salvation, when salvation is ours already as a gift. Works of service, however grand, are merely our ways of saying thanks.

I like what Janice Brewi has to say about wisdom rooted in religious experience in the book she co-authored with Anne Brennan, *Celebrate Mid-Life: Jungian Archetypes and Mid-Life Spirituality*[16] She says that one's life work can become a religious experience, when our whole being is involved in and dedicated to what we want to achieve. She sees work as archetypal. And she quotes

Teilhard de Chardin, that astounding contemporary mystic, to support her claim:

"God awaits us," Teilhard says, "every instant in our action, in the work of the moment. There is a sense in which he is at the tip of my pen, my spade, my brush, my needle—of my heart and of my thought." How can we speak of our work as part of growing older when the real task that seems to lie in front of us is letting go of work, letting go of our longing to supervise, to direct and control?[17]

To some of us it is given to work, actively, into our seventies and eighties. George Bernard Shaw began his playwriting career in his fifties and concluded it in his nineties. J.C. Penney wrote spiritual memoirs based on his business experience well into his eighties. Some of us keep the necessary physical strength to keep on working in our seventies as we were doing in our fifties and sixties.

It is well to remember that the work of reflection is also valuable work. Eula, my dear Eula, hit a serious health snag when she was in her late seventies, one that required her to leave the home she loved and take up residence in a nursing home. Cheerfully, she occupied half a room, condensing the belongings of a lifetime into relatively few, though the books and papers did seem to overflow.

At our suggestion—my mother's and mine—she bravely, and with enormous powers of recollection—began to write her memoirs! Abundantly, the loose-leaf pages came by mail, written in her large, clear, unmistakable hand, detailing events long past, country childhood memories, memories of young people's gatherings in New Orleans, marriage, family anecdotes, even an account of the Era Club of the 1920s in which she and others had been active for women's suffrage.

God was at the heart of her letting go. That simple fidelity to him, that childlike trust she had known from the beginning became more so in her last years, focused, as Hammer says, to pinpoints. She knew what mattered most.

Eula's pinpoints were intense moments of family feeling. God and family were ultimately the ones for whom she lived, and passionately. As she came closer to ninety she was more and more grateful for the beauty of her life, and told me often what a wonderful life she had had.

"To sum up," says the wise spiritual counselor, Jean-Pierre de Caussade, in his book, *Abandonment to Divine Providence*, "We must be active in all that the present moment demands of us, but in everything else remain passive and abandoned and do nothing but peacefully await the promptings of God."[18]

THE CHRIST-STORY BLOOMS AGAIN

"Every day will be an Easter," says one of the hymns I learned in childhood. Is every day a Christmas, too? From my postcard box I retrieve one that I discovered in the Atlanta airport with a photograph of dark red dogwood blooms. It tells me "The Legend of the Dogwood." It seems that the dogwood, being a firm, strong tree the size of the oak, was chosen for the purpose of the Crucifixion. Jesus, nailed upon the cross, sensed the tree's distress and said to it, "Because of your pity for my suffering, henceforth the Dogwood tree shall be slender, its blossoms in the form of a cross, two long and two short petals. The center of the outer edge of each petal will have rusted, blood stained nail prints. The center of the flower will be a crown of thorns and all who see it will remember." The legend reminds me of the ways we storytellers can experience both crucifixion and resurrection again and see them flower in our lives. Even when (especially when) historical facts are scanty, devotion thrives on legends and makes the Christ-story present to us where we are: in airports as well as on country lanes where dogwood bursts into bloom. The postcard—and the dogwood itself, when I am lucky enough to be present in earth-places where it flowers, are reminders to me that we are Easter people. When Gerard Manley Hopkins says we can let

Christ "easter in us," he adds something important. This eastering can occur in the darkness of our lives. Christ can be a "dayspring to the dimness in us."[19] Easter is the dawning of a transformed consciousness, a new way of seeing. When we ourselves live the story, new legends burst into bloom.

A year or two ago a woman I scarcely knew asked me to be part of her Maundy Thursdaying. At her invitation I took part in a washing of the feet with others in her circle, a liturgy designed to express their sense of the Easter message. When I took my shoe off and dipped my foot into the basin, I understood the grace of this moment for me—something this younger woman could not have anticipated. How could she have known (having me on a pedestal as she did) that I was so in need of healing? Could she have guessed that I was the one whose gimpy foot had been brutalized by the overcommitment of my life? Her gesture healed me, if not of my limp, then at least of some of my unwillingness to be attentive to my own needs. A small example? Yes. But larger healings and breakthroughs come about through the same loving openness to grace, the same kind of attentiveness to the Lord's presence in our lives. Another friend, a man, is mugged at gunpoint and lives to tell about it. He understands that his death-blow is a life-blow, an opportunity to live, even a reprieve, a chance to live differently, from now on. What is even more Jesus-like is his willingness to forgive the oppressors, to work for better living conditions for those who go out of their way to kill him.

SUFFERING AS TRANSFORMATION

As I get older, my own preoccupation is with healing on a larger scale. If individuals can be healed through their conscious contact with God, is the same breakthrough possible in communities, peoples, and nations? For a long time it has been possible for us in the West to look down from a pinnacle of affluence or comfort at "the poorer nations," to feel compassionate towards the poor and marginalized simply because they were overseas. Now the crumbling infrastructure is upon us and we are conscious that the whole system which we depend on is at risk. Problematic events converge—poor law enforcement, the drug crisis, racketeering, drug dealing, violence in the streets—to help us understand our peril. We who are already weak and frail must learn sacrifice for the sake of those even more helpless than ourselves. This is our cross, and in this suffering we will be transformed.

"By his stripes we are healed." In such a large scale task, the stripes of the suffering Servant of Isaiah will become ours. The flogging, the humiliation of our society's predicament, these times of suffering will no doubt be the making of us. But we need a kind of poetic vision, one that comes in the midst of darkness, to see the presence of God among us, leading us along the holy path. We need sprigs of dogwood—in airports, on country lanes—to know that God is eastering in us and that our sufferings are part of our transformation.

I like the way that Paul, writing to the Corinthians, finds metaphors in ordinary experience that disclose worlds of meaning. A little leaven leavens the whole lump. We who are believers have to become the new bread. Our paschal lamb has been sacrificed. We have to celebrate the Festival, not with the old leaven of evil, but with the new, unleavened bread of sincerity and truth. Living in the presence of God makes it possible for us to see new metaphors in our experience, metaphors that will change us if we are willing to live them. "Dying you destroyed our death; rising you restored our life. Lord Jesus, come in glory."

SIGNS OF RESURRECTION

Emily Dickinson lives close to death. She speaks of it as a neighbor, part of her everyday experience.

Because I could not stop for death
He kindly stopped for me;
The carriage held none but ourselves
And immortality.[20]

In Dickinson's day death is commonplace, something that happens in the parlor or in the dining room. So, too, with Charlotte, Emily, and Anne Brontë. In the Brontë parsonage at Haworth, one can be told in which precise parts of the room each member of the Brontë family died. Oddly, this nearness to death produces in these believers not despair but a clearer consciousness of the life to come.

But here and there are hints of resurrection. One surprise of the last year is that my son Henry (twenty-four) so sharply resembles my father, whom he hardly knew. When Henry was two-and-a-half my father dubbed him "El Rojo" because of his masses of red curls. A month later my father died. There was, over the ensuing twenty years, very little storytelling about him, nothing to make Norman Dietrich as alive to Henry as he inevitably was to me. A decade ago, in his teens, Henry met my uncle Warren, my father's youngest brother, and grasped a bit of what it was to be a Dietrich. Yet, there is no way that Henry could have taken on the nature of his Dietrich grandfather by imitation or a sense of the tradition. Instead, Henry's Dietrich streak came as a revelation to everyone, including himself. We were unprepared for the Norman-ness of the young man coming of age. All at once, it seemed, Henry matured: as raconteur, performer, film enthusiast, comic, debater par excellence, cultural observer, and clown. At first the secret could hardly be spoken. My mother noticed it, but wondered if she was the only one who had. Gradually I mustered up courage to mention it. "Do you see it, too?" "Absolutely!" What made it so curious was that Henry's coloring—fair white skin and brilliant red hair, worn, often, at shoulder-length during the time I speak of—was at odds with the Ned Dietrich of my memory, a man of suits, ties, and Humphrey Bogart snap-brim fedoras, preoccupied with cars, tires, carburetors, gasoline stations. When I call up a mind-picture of my father I see him, circa 1940, standing with one foot up on the running board of an old Chevy, his white shirt open slightly at the collar, tie tugged loose, a seersucker jacket flung over his shoulder, his arm moving up to wipe his face perspiring from the Louisiana heat.

Unmistakably, Norman Dietrich was present again in my son: in the opinions, the contentiousness, the love of picking a quarrel, the radical left-wing politics; alive too in the love of dancing, of night life, of New Orleans music; in joining a Carnival marching group (racially mixed, mind you!) that calls itself the Furious Five; in strutting, tossing the red hair, laughing, grinning, clowning; hogging the dance floor at Cafe Brazil in the Faubourg Marigny while his friends the Klezmer All-Stars perform; making a living in video stores and pizza joints and coffee houses while he struggles to become a screenwriter, novelist, film critic, movie director—all of these! Almost at once, everyone saw it: "He's so much like Norman Dietrich!"

Yes, this is Norman Dietrich's grandson! In Henry's voice, his movements, the jut of his jaw, the flash of his eyes, the suddenness of his laughter, the crazy, entertaining skew of his ideas, his love of speculation, his ability to reflect: all these are my father; are they also myself? All along I had been seeing him, as everyone else had, as Bill Griffin's son and almost-double. Everyone has seen that from the beginning: the joking, the love of books and reading, the storytelling, the dramatic imagination, the high romantic streak. Now that the cards are dealt out for another generation I see in Henry that the man I married, his father, is my father, too, in some unaccountable way I never saw before.

Where does yesterday leave off and tomorrow begin? In our children we are confronted time and again with mystery. How could this amazing thing happen, that people who are not ourselves are in some astounding way definitely us? Probably one of the best things about my father was that he was fun-loving. I vividly remember him seizing an umbrella to re-enact the drama of my mother's Uncle Sid and his way of walking down a street. In the same way my father loved to imitate the marching antics of the Jefferson City Buzzards, a Mardi Gras marching society. Now Henry lives the dream again, in ways my father's generation could never have imagined. And my father was pro-civil rights, so much so that he had the house in an uproar constantly with his "Yankee ideas." Is political liberalism transmitted in the genes? I would surely have blamed it on nurture, not nature!

Getting older is not only surrendering the past but giving way to the future. As if in a series of strobe-pictures I see Henry at fourteen, sixteen, eighteen, walking into manhood and the new maturity that sits comfortably in my mother's parlor, wolfing down chicken chow mein, conversing with a very new vocabulary ("What's been going on?") riffling through the *New York Times Book Review*, working up the last-minute cash to pay his rent, lingering pleasantly, then hurrying away. "He's so handsome!" my mother says after he has gone. The ache in my heart deepens, as I feel the weight of my dreams for him, my hopes for his happiness, my gratitude for his love and friendship.

All my children are my friends! Friends is a pale word for the affection I feel, the loyalty they give me, the steadfastness. I am praying for the strength to loose them, leave them free, drifting on water like Oscar's camellias, fresh, fragile, very beautiful. To see my children grow up is to be awestruck. In them I contemplate wonders I could not have invented or created: the uniqueness of people deeply like me, yet wonderfully themselves, held together by laughter, driven from within by the power of a mysterious, mostly unspoken love.

ALTERNATING MOODS:
CONTEMPLATION AND REFLECTION

In the garden of the Women's Faculty Club on the Berkeley campus, University of California, I find myself surrounded by roses. They are taller than I am. I have to stand on tiptoe to look at them. Big, tall on their stalks, secured by high sticks, their wide velvet petals curl exquisitely. I am sure God must have thought of them: not only the roses but each detail of their conduct, their seductiveness, their queenliness, their desire to compete, brilliant reds rivalling bright yellows, deep pinks with petals that diminish to pale edges; all three varieties standing high and reaching up for sun.

They are outrageous. But over the way from them is an equal outrage: one oversized white hydrangea bloom, ample, balanced to perfection, dozens of small, hesitant, round petals trembling on silly stems, arranged in formal harmony.

I am reminded of Avery Dulles' moment of conversion at the budding young tree on the River Charles. Then a Harvard undergraduate, Dulles came out of Widener Library where he had been reading St. Augustine and wrestling with the question of God. On the riverbank, in what he took to be the tree's obedience, Dulles, in one burst of insight, saw God. The insight was so persuasive that it brought him, that same evening, to pray. What does my own moment of insight require of me? Is my dialogue with the flowers already a kind of prayer?

Not to mention the ferns. They are robust and fresh. A slate path leads down into shade, going where? From my top-story window I have seen a tall man, handsomely suited in blue, descend and disappear, his white hair so coifed that his hair-do proclaims him the servant of fashion, not indifferent to sex, even possibly vain? (What is this place of such affluence that even the scholars are stylish?) I, Sherlock Holmes, say by means of detection that this fellow on the garden-path is Narcissus grown old. He likes his reflection in the mirror and though he is old a certain self-conscious desire to please can be seen as he walks. I say this without hesitation even though my eyes from the upper window catch just a snapshot of him. I am old, and still dancing; he is old, and still mincing. What shall I make of this sound of fiddles tuning up that constantly says to my heart that something is not ending but starting? Young or not, love is the energy that drives the universe. Always, even though it be not sex but spirit, the dance is about to begin.

Behind the house a garden, pleasingly round and green, invites the studious heart. Here harmony is, and wholeness, detachment and freedom. In the past I have come to scholarly meetings completely enslaved by my passions, to win, to control, to dominate. Who was I, in that other time? Why should I feel so different now, yet wary that these passions may assault me again? With detachment I can live within the dimension of roses, inhabit the hydrangea's circumference, I can blow and tremble with the blue flowers that bloom along the college roads. With the pyracantha and the ivy I will proclaim the beauty of God. I have grown wise like the palms of Berkeley and Engedi.

Two kinds of experience dominate me now: contemplation and reflection. Breakfasting after my Berkeley conference, I have talked with a clump of scholars about the transformation of society; one of them, a professor of philosophy at Boston College, has given me a clue in my research. From his kindness and the high compliment he pays me in the dialogue, my spirit soars. I am a writer! I am a scholar! My old age will be the crown of life! In our witty badinage I have reminded him that Cato learned Greek at eighty. He has responded, "Touché." I thank God for his reminder of the things I love in scholarship and intellectual life. Cicero's essay *On Old Age* is one of them! The climb I have made up the wearisome steps of my existence, to this point where the years ahead must be the last, this is not sad but serious; filled with meaning, not the hot promise and potential of youth, not the crunch and clatter of middle life, but something more contemplative, more reflective: at the top of the staircase, a small door leads into the upper reaches of Wisdom. In that tower Rapunzel will at last let down her hair.

CHAPTER ELEVEN

Homeward

O ne way to celebrate the present moment is by making a beautiful space in the week for friends and visiting. Such a moment comes for Bill and me when we invite our friends Colette and Jim Stelly and Pouff and Richard Jaubert to have brunch with us.

Have we taken leave of our senses? We have decided to serve soufflé! Why such audacity? What would move us to risk serving such a menu to seasoned travelers who go to France often and are of French background themselves?

Perhaps the fact that I am a native of New Orleans gives me courage. I have grown up with good food, and loving to cook seems second nature. Today, the restaurant fare of New Orleans is even more diverse and pleasing than in my childhood. We have created our own cosmopolitan cuisine. Cooking at home gives me a chance to celebrate this culture, to share the riches of my own heritage. Also, when money is tight, as it is for two writers who are stretching to cover life-commitments, having friends in makes it possible to have the elegance of a great restaurant in one's own dining room.

So we have invited good friends (neighbors!) to Sunday brunch. Colette is actually a professor of French. Her doctorate, earned late, is in the teaching of languages. She goes to France often, sometimes taking Pouff along with her; they know both French and Louisiana cuisine well. And their husbands are equally critical! Richard, Pouff, and Jim are genuine Creoles. Richard and Pouff are New Orleans natives (her real name is Marie-Elise, but everyone calls her Pouff) who have traveled in Europe often. Jim, a native of Opelousas, comes from a French family that has been in Louisiana at least two centuries. He has lived in New Orleans most of his life and works as a travel agent, with many opportunities to see the best of English and European life.

I, on the other hand, am an American of English and German descent, whose only pretense to French cooking is a lifetime of reading *The Joy of Cooking* and various books by Julia Child.

My motive is clear: something in my character loves to live on the edge. Making soufflé is a kind of pirouette in the hot glare of center stage, a risk-taking bid for deafening applause. Looked at another way, it is my quest for perfection, a high celebration of the beauty of created things. Soufflé is a theological statement, a religious affirmation. God is good! Le bon dieu has given us the imagination to create soufflé.

Perhaps, also, the house we live in demands soufflé, as it demands flowers and civility in profusion. Ours is an old house, a raised Creole cottage that has weathered many hurricanes. The ceilings are sixteen feet high. In the front of the house is a long, beautiful room, previously a double parlor, no doubt, with high windows overlooking the street and side garden. In this room are two fireplaces. The walls are deep red and the draperies a sort of bone. On the walls are oil portraits of my Louisiana ancestors, Nathaniel Evans, Lucy Adelaide Foley and her daughter Lucy Adelaide Evans; Nathaniel Evans is alone in his portrait, wearing a high formal collar of the early 1800s. Family tradition has it that his picture was made in London after he made money as a Louisiana cotton planter and returned to his native country.

WHERE THE HEART IS

What is the occasion? We are in search of Sunday. All through the winter and spring we have been forced, by the economics of our lives, to work all seven days of the week, believing all the while in the importance of Sunday as the Lord's day. Yet we are working to keep this beautiful house and our lives in it from being swept away. What could be more important, then, than Sunday at home, Sunday with dear friends around us, Sunday with a menu that honors their friendship in some celebratory way.

My husband is the one who loves to set the table and to see the house appointed with flowers; the books that generally overflow in every corner of library and living room must be gathered into some sort of pattern, not too accidental, not too planned. We decide to use our wedding china and silver, our crystal glasses. Bill has chosen a good Chardonnay and has chilled several bottles of Perrier as well. He plans the music also, choosing from our somewhat antiquated library of long-playing records a few that seem just right.

I have the presence of mind to put all the ingredients out, bringing my eggs, milk, and cheese to room temperature. As I grate the cheese my daughter comes in and begins to admire the well-tempered kitchen, more organized, perhaps, than on the ordinary days of our lives. She is making honey mustard dressing for a salad she will take to her job at the film house two blocks away. Sarah packs her salad into a refrigerator dish, leaving half the honey mustard dressing behind. I will use this for my guests, I think.

The guests are invited for noon. At eleven o'clock I begin to be afraid of running short: of cookies to serve with the fruit that Colette is bringing, of time to prepare everything well. I try to send Bill to the store for the cookies I have in mind. He refuses to go. "What if they don't have what you're looking for? You should be the one who goes," he insists. I see it his way and hurry to the store, where I pluck the extra head of lettuce, the croutons, the shortbread to accompany the fruit compote Colette will bring. Bill was right. In fact, the store no longer has the brand of cookies I wanted, and I spend precious minutes looking for others (not too expensive) that will measure up to the meal.

Returning to the house, breathless, I become a quick-change artist, slipping into a dress proper for both cooking and visiting. I discover that the apron is as much a part of my costume as the dress. Part of my joy on this beautiful day is the preparing. Anticipation is as precious as fulfillment.

Separating eggs takes skill; it delights me to discover that even when time is short, I do this well. Gradually, the whites collect in one deep bowl, while the yolks build up in another. I congratulate myself for being beyond the newlywed's hesitancy. I know how to cook!

Over the flame, the heat of the double boiler is measured, dependable. With a wooden spoon I stir the butter and flour together, gradually adding the cheese and milk and feel the exquisite drag on the spoon that means it is just right. In go the seasonings, dashes of salt and cayenne. Now the yolks create a golden texture.

Quick, beat the whites till they rise, fluffy and firm. I find myself remembering a former colleague, a master of the soufflé, who believed the whites should always be whipped by hand. I don't have the elbow strength: don't have it now, didn't have it then! But a terrible thought strikes after I have put my beater into the whites. What if I failed to wash the beater after beating the yolks? What if the whites don't rise?

From the front hallway, I hear the guests arriving. Bill knows that if I don't come out, it means I'm still coping with the kitchen. By now, it's a balancing act. Salad greens being washed, shaken dry, drained, broken into appetizing bite-sized pieces; juicy red Creole tomatoes, the best of the season, quartered; green onions cut; croutons added. In a large glass salad bowl, every color in the salad glows with life and appetite. I pour three different kinds of dressings into my favorite serving pieces: one is the mayonnaise-dish we got as a wedding gift almost thirty years before.

But the egg whites! This is my crucible for today. If the egg whites don't rise, there will be no soufflé. The beater whirs and whirs but I see no hope. The sticky mixture lies in the bowl, mocking my aspirations. I add cream of tartar, hoping for the ideal chemistry. Still, no apparent progress. Finally, as the beater keeps purring, it occurs to me to pray.

"Oh, I'm sure Emilie will come out and say hello in a few minutes... " I hear Bill making small talk in the front rooms.

Thank heaven my husband is a first-class wit. I am sure he will keep everyone thoroughly amused while I continue struggling with the egg whites. Bill is not so much a raconteur as a wicked man with a punch line. His humor, both in his writing and conversation, is known far and wide. Lucky for me in my struggle with the egg whites.

At last, they do rise, doubling and tripling under my astonished gaze. I begin thanking God, as I pour the yolk mixture in, then fill the souffle-dishes and slide them into the oven. Again, I have forgotten to pre-heat the oven soon enough. I'll have to trust God to compensate for the oven temperature as well.

As I walk from the kitchen to the front of the house, the joyful sound of small talk falls on my ears. Pouff and Colette are telling their husbands that Bill and Emilie were brilliant in their recent talk.... We bask in the approval they give us. Bill serves me a chilled Perrier. I am starting to relax and appreciate camaraderie. On a chair near me, beside the fireplace, Colette's deep pink straw hat, brimming with outrageous flowers, symbolizes all the joy and civility I aspire to. Pouff and Bill are engaged in one of their high tweaking sessions. I know that when Bill is teasing her about the antiquarian charm of the ladies's club she belongs to he is secretly planning to use the club in some short story or novel he will write! From the kitchen, I hear a reassuring sound. The stove rings to tell me the soufflé is ready. After a mad dash down the hallway—I discover that the soufflés have risen to perfection, a crusty golden brown.

With baguettes, fresh butter, iced Chardonnay, Perrier, salad, and three kinds of salad dressing, we are ready to sit down. Bill calls everyone to the table. He has written them place cards. The table has a centerpiece of six flags—the six flags under which we have lived in the history of New Orleans.

Bill says grace, from his grab-bag box of graces. Wine and water are poured, and our celebration is complete. Around the table, the bonds of spiritual friendship are strong. Richard, sitting to my left, tells me about his Creole childhood in New Orleans. Everyone praises my soufflé, and Richard says it reminds him of one of their favorite restaurants in the South of France.

For an hour or so, there is a sense of time suspended. The clocks have stopped ticking and we float in contentment and civility. God, it seems to us, is at the center: of who we are, and the way we live and love.

Our guests have gone by three o'clock. But we move in a dream, prolonging the joy. Washing up goes easily. Carefully handling and putting away each plate or spoon gives us time with each other, to enjoy the time just spent, to relive the conversations we have had.

On Wednesday, Colette's thank you note comes, and it's a tour-de-force:

The Official Gault Millau rating of Griffin's Bistro:

Le Crêpe Nanou and the Upperline, two popular uptown restaurants, ought to take heed lest Emilie Griffin, their close neighbor and noted chef, show them up. Actually, Griffin's Bistro is a family-run operation, which accounts for its consistent quality and highly personal touch. At our last visit chez Griffin's, Emilie and husband Bill turned out a French déjeuner which was pure delight. After aperitifs, guests were seated in the dining room at a table complete with white linen, international flags, crystal lamps, and a center piece of freshly baked baguettes. The main course consisted of a garden fresh salade composée with a choice of house dressings, and a golden brown cheese soufflé. We needed only one taste of the soufflé to know that a certain bistro in Paris in the rue Tabor, which specializes in these airy concoctions, would be proud to lay claim to Emilie's ethereal creation. Complementing this was a crisp white Chardonnay. Dessert, consisting of macedoine de fruits and gateau secs, was followed by coffee and continued stimulating conversation. We wish to compliment the chef and her trusty staff for this perfectly orchestrated summer dining experience. (Signed) Colette H. Stelly for Christian Millau.

IN THE MIDST OF EVERYTHING, LONGING

I come at last to *homewardness*, a sort of theology of my own devising, based on an experience that is commonplace, I would almost say universal. It is that kind of ordinary anguish which we sometimes call homesickness and sometimes by another name, a longing for what is not, a restlessness of the heart. It is an experience so fundamentally human that, however little we may have suffered from it ourselves (possibly some have not confronted it, yet I suspect this yearning is embedded in their hearts) we nevertheless find it easy to recognize and identify with in another person. We know at once how E.T. felt when he missed his home planet and thought he could never return. A chord is touched in us when we hear: "E.T. phone home."

True homesickness is a very particular and limited experience which comes when things familiar and beloved are snatched away: when the child is taken from her mother, when the native is driven from his homeland. What follows is that kind of exile and dislocation so often called by contemporary writers "alienation." The writer Walker Percy speaks of the human condition as that of a castaway. The wistful character of America's immigrant experience and ethnic cultures may come from this nostalgia for a lost homeland, the country idealized in memory to which the exiles can never return.

How, on the other hand, to account for the homesickness which has no immediate, proximate cause in our life-circumstances? What about our nostalgia for something we don't fully remember, a longing for something else, something more, not fully focused, not entirely concrete? We sense that something is missing, something that ought to be but isn't, some fulfillment which no earthly achievement can ever furnish or supply. What we and the poets feel as something "lost" may be a memory not of the past but the future: a "memory" of something yet to be given, something that can't be fully grasped in the life we live now.

Can we build a theology on this longing for something that is not yet, a prompting that tells us we are strangers here, travelling to our home country, our rightful home? Can we build on this metaphor so deeply embedded in our poetry and our prayers? "To thee do we cry, poor banished children of Eve, to thee do we send up our sighs, mourning and weeping in this valley of tears."

This is the God we run to: the lover beyond all loves who will satisfy our deepest longing, will nourish us with apples and cradle us in his lap. This is the God who exactly matches the God-space within each of us. The philosopher and theologian Bernard Lonergan has said it well: "There lies within (the person's) horizon a region for the divine, a shrine for ultimate holiness. It cannot be ignored. The atheist may pronounce it empty. The agnostic may urge that he finds his investigation has been inconclusive. The contemporary humanist will refuse to allow the question to arise. But their negations presuppose the spark in our clod, our native orientation to the divine."

The answer to this inner question, this empty space, is as simple as being-in-love-with-God. Lonergan says that such fulfillment "brings a deep-set joy that can remain despite humiliation, failure, privation, pain, betrayal, desertion. That fulfillment brings radical peace, the peace that the world cannot give."[1]

From my own experience I would add confirming notes, corollaries to Lonergan's interpretation.

- First, the "click" of recognition we feel when the idea of God is presented to us. God is a person whose nature and existence we comprehend without explanation, as though a name were being given to a being we already know. The mention of God corresponds to a longing we already know.

- Second, the spontaneous flowering of belief in all times and places, in all sorts of societies, the prevalence of the notion of God in our speech, even in the speech of the unbeliever, an idea which is often stamped on or thrust aside, to be sure, but a hardy perennial nonetheless.

- Third, and this is of the greatest importance, the experience of destination which seems to gather momentum with each passing year, so that as our physical faculties decline, we sense ourselves moving toward an unseen goal, gathering speed, even being quickened by the possibility of something yet to come.

There is a match between us and God. The match makes sense. It has an inner coherence. Yet this is not the stuff for argument, for analysis. This is the stuff of the graced imagination.

It is time to pray, to put our feeble faith-imagination into play, to put ourselves in the presence of God. The older we get, the more we know that we are in the Lord's presence already, and to know him face-to-face is only a matter of time. What I called longing or desire is really a drive, a thrust towards God, our ultimate destiny, our destination. Faith in Lonergan's description, is the experience of God's love flooding our hearts, our unrestricted thrust to self-transcendence, our orientation towards the mystery of love and awe. So we perceive it, not only in the overwhelming joy of first conversion, but in all the conversions of our lives, in the fervor of an intense prayer life, in the privileged moments of our love-affair with God.

But the kingdom is not yet, never fully present this side of the boundary. Everything is a hope, a presumption, a prefiguring, a preliminary knowing, a kind of guesswork through grace. The longing remains even when we are most aware of God, when the experience of God is embedded in our hearts. When this Lord of ours is most intensely, intimately close there is still something yet to be given, an emptiness and a hunger for what is yet to be. This love, like Shakespeare's elusive passion, is too dear for our possessing; but again, paraphrasing Shakespeare, it's like enough God knows his estimate.[2]

> Will thou show wonders to the dead?
> Shall the dead arise and praise thee?
> Shall thy lovingkindness be declared in the grave?
> Or thy faithfulness in destruction?
> Shall thy wonders be known in the dark?
> And thy righteousness in the land of forgetfulness?[3]

THE LAUGHTER OF RESURRECTION

One of the paintings I love is by the English artist Stanley Spencer. It is oil on canvas and hangs in the Tate Gallery in

London. I have only seen it once, when it was on loan to the Guggenheim museum in New York. It depicts the general resurrection and is called "The Resurrection, Cookham."

In this painting the moment we have all waited for is at hand. The resurrected folk of Cookham are climbing out of their narrow spaces, wearing the dress of various centuries as the earth bursts into bloom. The picture is impossibly naïve. So, too, must we be.

Whenever I see this picture—I have a small postcard reproduction that is part of my devotions—I want to laugh out loud. Resurrection is so totally absurd! I know that our human imagination cannot fully grasp it. It is beyond us; God has something else, something far beyond our human imagination, in store.

Getting older doesn't have to be learned; it simply happens. But to live it with grace is a kind of learning, which, like all learning, is painful. Learning how to let go of all that has gone before, to live memories for the sake of others instead of merely for ourselves, to let go of mastery, to take smaller steps; to dwell in the instant; to experience the collapse of time.

"I won't be here the next time you come, Emilie," I remember as my mother-in-law's last words to me. Remembering this, I see myself standing beside the hospital bed, summoning up the will to leave her. I remember the smile, the china blue eyes, the intensity. In that moment I was swamped by her detachment, her readiness, her acceptance of what had to be. I wondered if I could ever let go so fully, so gamely, from the life I treasure as my own.

Now, with my mother, I move from chair to door frame, from bath to kitchen, from bed to table, in a moment-to-moment process that prefigures my own uncertain future. Sometimes our love of theater, sometimes our playfulness sustains us as nothing else does.

"Stand up straight," I find myself telling her. "I don't want you to lose your balance. Be the Empress Helena when you enter the room." She is the leading lady. I am, at least for the moment, directing the play.

"If I am the Empress Helena," she says, "I command you to bring me a glass of ice."

And we laugh about that.

JOURNEYS END IN LOVERS' MEETINGS

As I move through the small tasks and lazinesses that mark my nights and my days, a relentless dialogue with the Lord continues. Words are recited silently and these are expressions of affirmation and hope. With your right hand you hold me, you comfort me. Fear is the enemy and I know it. I hold the Lord to his word: You prepare a table before me in the presence of my enemies. You anoint my head with oil. My writerliness plays with the Bible language: Only with my eyesight will I behold the reward of the wicked. I visualize, romanticize, synthesize, re-memorize: For you will give your angels charge over me, to keep me in all my ways. They will bear me up in their hands, lest I dash my foot against a stone.

The voyage continues, and the destination, even though beyond us, is informed by a kind of faith-confidence; we have become used to the open sea, expecting the Lord to bring us home to the place we are heading for. In the rigging somewhere we will decipher the face of Jesus Christ; or even if we do not spy him, we will know that he has gone ahead of us, the dayspring, the way-shower, the fellow-sufferer who understands, God sharing our condition and transforming it. The Lord God takes hold and brings us closer to the far horizon of our future. Dawn is stealing over the rim of the world and bringing us close to fulfillment, the knowledge of who we are and where we belong. No more will we have to be castaways. We will come home at last, in some unexplained but resolute way. I think it is something like Thor Heyerdal's raft, the Kon-Tiki, after long weeks in the Pacific swells, coming nearer to its destination. After a very long time of drifting in silence, a loud, sudden noise will shortly come from the sea birds around us, creatures who have come to tell us the dangers are over, we have come through. The moon will hang large and round; it will welcome us with a hot, even a sun-like yellow shine, even though its light is no more than a reflection of the glory yet to come. A faint, violet-blue veil over the sky will give way, by degrees, to a ruddy glow, and then, on the horizon, something like a blue pencil line.

Land.

APPENDIX

Exercises

G etting older is a task for spirituality. In all spiritualities there are exercises, and these are to be commended. Those that I mention here are perhaps not spiritual exercises in the conventional sense, but rather ways toward integration. Faithfully practiced, creatively applied, they may help us draw together the diverse strands of our lives into what we hope to see, reflectively, as a whole.

1. **Make pilgrimages.** Don't believe that you will fail to have lived if you don't get to Paris or Rome. The fullness of God is available everywhere. But if some part of yourself is not at peace because of a time and place in your life that should be revisited, do it by all means. Don't hesitate to ask the current resident of your childhood home whether you can re-enter and see the old staircase where you once played hide and seek. Approach the experience prayerfully. Prepare for the possibility of tears.

2. **Seek out old friends and forgive old enemies.** I was astonished, when I tried to start forgiving my enemies, to realize how

many loose ends were trailing in my life. I am still attempting to identify and forgive the persons against whom I have harbored annoyances and resentments. To forgive an old enemy does not necessarily require renewing the friendship on the same terms or failing to learn from past mistakes. But to re-encounter and forgive is cleansing and part of a life's possibility of integration and wisdom.

3. **Attend reunions.** A certain kind of spiritual courage is required to attend reunions. To attend class reunions is to learn that some of our number have already died, and others may be in danger of dying soon. What is more critical is that some have achieved more than others, some have lost their looks, others their money or prestige. Reunions require of us that we understand how to let go of harsh interpersonal competitiveness, forgive ourselves for what we have not done, and stop counting the dimensions of other people's swimming pools. The Ten Commandments are useful; thou shalt not covet thy neighbor's mergers or acquisitions; thou shalt overlook thy neighbor's bankruptcies.

4. **Make deliberate efforts to let your children go.** Choosing new ways to visit with them as peers, over the lunch table, at the coffee house, and the like, emphasizes the new framework of the relationship. This is not the same as "down-nesting," encouraging your children to move out. The delicate, difficult, and most desirable goal is a renegotiated relationship with children as adults. Recognize how much you have done that they must forgive you for; forget it; forgive it; move on.

5. **Reevaluate, renovate, and restage holidays.** Holidays are, in my view, the most perilous days in family life. These are the times when parents most long to possess their children, stuffing them back into the teddy-bear costumes they once wore. A

spiritual exercise may consist in asking the children to plan Thanksgiving or Christmas and accepting their suggestions with enthusiasm and creativity. Assess your own weaknesses and strengths in the new relationships by the simplicity and understatement you bring to the new situation of having grown children (whether or not they live away from home.)

6. **In a relationship with an older relative or friend, one whose life is reaching its term, celebrate and rejoice in the achievements and pleasures of what has happened up to now.** I was fortunate to have an early warning of my mother's declining health, one that permitted me to organize a celebration of her long, fifty-year entrepreneurial career. I will always be grateful to God for the opportunity to do this—at an elegant event sponsored by the New Orleans Board of Trade. A less elaborate event, however, would have accomplished the same aim: to celebrate, gratefully, a gifted life and a generous giver.

7. **Organize, if possible, a significant journey.** I was moved by a newspaper account by a woman who took her aging mother on a journey through Europe.[1] She took her mother from a nursing home in the Middle West and took her along on a complex European journey. Though her mother's memory was failing, and she could not retain memories of, or even perhaps fully appreciate, places she was passing through, what mattered was the companionship between mother and daughter. It was a holy journey and an opportunity for the daughter's spiritual regeneration. "Then again, her thoughts would drift into places I'd never before heard her mention. For example, she told me how on some summer mornings when she was a child, her father would hitch up the horse and buggy, the kids would pile in, and they'd all drive out to a spot called Mint Springs, at the foot of a hill that mounted steeply all tangled with mint and other greenery. A kind of paradise,

she remembered." The mother and daughter were not religious. Still, it seems that they knew about paradise! Especially when her mother says, "I'll bet Mint Springs is standing just as it was somewhere around here."

8. **Plan family reunions.** If it is impractical to have family reunions, reconstruct the experience through sharing of photographs and memorabilia. Take out the albums and leaf through them. Make occasions to do so, and to add to them. Tell stories as you do.

9. **Weave family rituals.** Tell stories and hand on traditions. Be sure that in the development of family rituals, you include the creativity of the youngest members, and allow for activities that will amuse them. There is nothing more counterproductive than boring children with the least interesting things about the past.

10. **Write memoirs.** It is an act of faith to write memoirs. As anyone knows who has been interviewed by a younger person about some historical experience from the past, to write one's memoirs is to admit one's own frailty and the time-limits of one's life. This requires courage as well as creativity. To do it joyfully is to live one's faith, and to set a good example of how to face old age and death.

11. **Encourage older members of the family to write memoirs.** If there is someone whose memories you cherish, who can't organize the project, help him or her to do it. Make tape-recordings. Plan interview guides. Think up topics to prompt memories. Experience the flow of memory and time as a spiritual gift to you, and to others, through you.

12. **Become a letter-writer if you can.** Include, in your writing, to the extent that it is natural and appropriate, your faith in God. Your letters will become a spiritual journey and a spiritual exercise.

13. **Engage in some effort for the transformation of society.** Churches, clubs, learned societies, groups dedicated to the handing on of tradition, all these may work to strengthen the social fabric. Perhaps, however, there is some group that is dedicated to your own vision of the good and which is pursuing it in a modest, diligent, and realistic way. Whether at the level of policy or the simpler level of volunteering, seize the chance to work with them as your resources permit. "It is all that is good, everything that is perfect, which is given us from above; it comes down from the Father of all light; with him there is no such thing as alteration, no shadow of a change."[2] By involvement in the social good we act as doers of the word, not hearers only.

NOTES

To the Reader

1. Wisdom 14:1-6. Unless otherwise indicated, Scripture citations are from *The Jerusalem Bible*.

TWO
Memory Travels with Us

1. Truman Capote, *A Christmas Memory* (New York: Random House, 1956), 12.
2. Emilie Griffin, *The Only Begotten Son*, unpublished playscript, author's copyright, 1971, 7.
3. Erik H. Erikson, *The Life Cycle Completed: A Review*. (New York: W.W. Norton Company, 1982). See especially chapter 3, 58-62.
4. Erikson, 58-62.
5. Proverbs 3:24, author's paraphrase.
6. Matthew 11:28.
7. Matthew 6:33-34a.
8. Matthew 7:8.
9. Viktor E. Frankl, *Man's Search for Meaning* (New York: Washington Square Press, 1963), 56.
10. Karl Rahner, "Theology and Anthropology," in *Theological Investigations*, vol. IX (New York: The Seabury Press, 1976), 41.
11. G.K. Chesterton, *The Catholic Church and Conversion* (New York: The Macmillan Company, 1961), 64.
12. William James, *The Varieties of Religious Experience* (Toronto, Ontario: The Macmillan Company, 1961), 172, 177.
13. Augustine, *Confessions*, trans. Rex Warner. (New York: New American Library, 1963), Book VIII, chapter 12, 180.
14. C.S. Lewis, *Surprised by Joy: The Shape of My Early Life* (New York: Harcourt Brace Jovanovich, 1955), 230-1.

15. C.S. Lewis, *God in the Dock* (Grand Rapids, Mich.: Eerdmans, 1970), 261.
16. Lewis, *Surprised by Joy*, 180.
17. Lewis, *Surprised by Joy*, 27.
18. C.S. Lewis, *God in the Dock*, 261.

THREE
Prayer as Navigation

1. Song of Songs 2:11-12.
2. Kenneth Briggs, "America's Return to Prayer," *New York Times Magazine*, November 18, 1984.
3. Lewis, *Surprised by Joy*, 181.
4. Lewis, *Surprised by Joy*, 180.
5. See my book, *Clinging: The Experience of Prayer* (San Francisco: Harper & Row, 1984), (McCracken Press, 1994.) Not an instructional manual but a brief work inviting the reader to experience various moods of prayer.
6. John Henry Newman, "On Christian Repentance," in *Parochial and Plain Sermons*, vol. III, (London: Longmans, Green & Company, 1899), 90. Newman says: "The most perfect Christian is to himself but a beginner, a penitent prodigal, who has squandered God's gifts, and comes to him to be tried over again, not as a son but as a hired servant."
7. William Shakespeare, *Hamlet*, Act I, Scene iii, line 62, as it appears in Thomas Marc Parrott, ed., *Shakespeare: Twenty-Three Plays and the Sonnets*, (New York: Charles Scribner's Sons, 1938), 682.
8. John Donne, *Devotions upon Emergent Occasions*, Meditation XVII, in Alexander M. Witherspoon and Frank J. Warnke, eds. *Seventeenth Century Prose and Poetry*, (New York: Harcourt, Brace & World, 1963), 68.
9. "The Twelve Promises of Alcoholics Anonymous," New York, Alcoholics Anonymous World Service.

FOUR
Night Fears

1. Doris Lessing, *The Summer Before the Dark*, (New York: Bantam Books, 1978), 8.
2. John 8:51-52.
3. Romans 8:31.
4. Psalm 71:9, 14, 18.
5. Geoff Ryman, *Was* (New York: Penguin Books, 1993).
6. John Milton, *Paradise Lost*, Book I, line 254-5, found in Harry Francis Fletcher, ed., *The Complete Poetical Works of John Milton* (Boston: Houghton Mifflin, 1941), 160.
7. Isaiah 65:24, KJV.

FIVE
Watches of the Night

1. Thornton Wilder, *Our Town* (New York: Harper & Row Perennial Library, 1957), 82.
2. Emily Dickinson, "Resurgam," in *Favorite Poems of Emily Dickinson* (New York: Avenel Books, 1978), 141.
3. Henry Vaughan, "They Are All Gone into that World of Light," in Alexander M. Witherspoon and Frederick M. Warnke, eds., *Seventeenth Century Prose and Poetry*, 985-6.
4. See my book, *Chasing the Kingdom: a Parable of Faith*, (San Francisco: Harper San Francisco, 1990), for a treatment of St. Francisville as heaven, drawing creatively on the book of Revelation.
5. 1 Corinthians 13:12, author's paraphrase.
6. Matthew 6:21, KJV.

SIX
A Different Wisdom

1. C.S. Lewis, *The Weight of Glory and Other Addresses* (Grand Rapids, Mich.: Eerdmans, 1975), 14.
2. Isaiah 52:14.
3. Isaiah 53:2-3.
4. Isaiah 53:8, 7.
5. John 20:16-17.
6. Exodus 16:3.
7. Exodus 17:3.
8. John 14:5.
9. Psalm 119:25, 30-31.
10. 1 Peter 1:8-9, 10.
11. Sr. Marie Lenihan, CSJ, "Taking Life's Walk with the Elderly," Brooklyn *Tablet*.
12. Alfred Lord Tennyson, "Crossing the Bar," as it appears in Robert C. Pooley, et al., eds. *England in Literature*, (Chicago: Scott Foresman and Company, 1953), 401. The editors observe that Tennyson's phrase, "no moaning of the bar" is based on an old superstition, to the following effect. The outgoing tide sometimes moans as it rolls over an intervening sandbar. This was once believed to mean that a death had occurred.

SEVEN
Lands of Nod

1. Interview with Robert McGriff, in "Together Apart, The Myth of Race, Special Report, Part III," *The New Orleans Times-Picayune*, August 16, 1993, 1.

2. Galatians 3:28.
3. Galatians 4:6, 7.
4. Evelyn Eaton Whitehead and James D. Whitehead, *Christian Life Patterns: The Psychological Challenges and Religious Invitations of Adult Life* (New York: Crossroad, 1992), 130.
5. Mary's canticle, known as "The Magnificat," as it appears in Luke 1:46-55, KJV.
6. John Baillie, *Invitation to Pilgrimage* (Harmondsworth, Middlesex, England: Penguin Books, 1960), 126.
7. Judges 4:23.
8. Judges 5:20, KJV.
9. Psalm 20:7 KJV.
10. Psalm 44:5-6.
11. Jeremiah 50:33-34.
12. Psalm 127:1, KJV.
13. Baillie, *Invitation to Pilgrimage,* 127.
14. Luke 11:27-28.
15. Christina Rossetti, "A Christmas Carol," quoted in Linda Ching Sledge, *Shivering Babe, Victorious Lord: The Nativity in Poetry and Art,* (Grand Rapids, Mich.: William B. Eerdmans Publishing Company, 1981), 129.
16. Revelation 3:15-17.
17. Revelation 3:18-19.
18. Revelation 3:20, 22.
19. Charles Dickens, *A Christmas Carol* (New York: Holiday House, 1983), 105-106.

EIGHT
Wings of Morning

1. Letter from Angela Allen-Ostar of High Bridge, New Jersey, published in the *New York Times Sunday Magazine,* August 15, 1993. Allen-Ostar challenged Rona Berg's fashion feature, "The Model T's," which the magazine had published July 18, 1993.
2. Acts of the Apostles 17:28, KJV.
3. George Herbert, "Love," lines 1-6, as they appear in *A Choice of George Herbert's Verse,* selected with an introduction by R.S. Thomas (London: Faber & Faber, 1967), 91.
4. Griffin, *Clinging,* 43.
5. William Wordsworth, "Michael," in David Perkins, ed., *English Romantic Writers* (New York: Harcourt, Brace and World, 1967), 276.

NINE
Souls in Full Sail

1. Jean-Pierre de Caussade, *Abandonment to Divine Providence*, trans. John Beevers (New York: Doubleday, 1975), 50-51.
2. John Freccero, "Introduction," in John Ciardi, trans., *The Paradiso: Dante's Ultimate Vision of Universal Harmony and Eternal Salvation* (New York: New American Library, 1970), ix.
3. Ciardi, *The Paradiso*, Canto XXVII, lines 109-11, 301.
4. Frankl, *Man's Search for Meaning*, 58-59.
5. Sheridan Gilley, *Newman and His Age* (Westminster, Maryland: Christian Classics, 1990), 26.
6. This and citations from Hopkins' letters immediately following, appear in Gerard Manley Hopkins, *Poems and Prose*, selected and edited by W.H. Gardner (Harmondsworth, Middlesex, England: Penguin Books, 1963).
7. Hopkins, 51.
8. A.N. Wilson, *Eminent Victorians* (London, BBC Books, 1989), 161.
9. John Henry Newman, "The Calls of Grace," in *Faith and Prejudice* (New York: Sheed & Ward, 1956), 49.
10. From "The Golden Echo," *Gerard Manley Hopkins: Poems and Prose*, lines 26-32, 54.

TEN
Eastering

1. Hosea 11:1-2.
2. Hosea 11:3.
3. Hosea 11:4.
4. Hosea 11:5-6.
5. Hosea 11:8a.
6. Hosea 11:8b-9.
7. Luke 7:31-32.
8. Luke 8:10.
9. Luke 8:8.
10. Jim Forest, *Love Is the Measure* (New York: Paulist Press, 1986).
11. Luke 18:15-16.
12. Matthew 5:11-12.
13. See James McKay, *The Management of Time* (Englewood Cliffs, N.J.: Prentice-Hall, 1959), 71-75.
14. John Milton, *Paradise Lost*, see note 34.
15. Armand Hammer, *Hammer* (New York: G.P. Putnam's Sons, 1987), 468.
16. Janice Brewi and Anne Brennan, *Celebrate Mid-Life: Jungian Archetypes and Mid-Life Spirituality* (New York: Crossroad, 1988).
17. Teilhard de Chardin, passage from *The Divine Milieu* (New York: Harper & Row, 1960), quoted in *Celebrate Mid-Life*, 248-49.

18. De Caussade, 79.
19. Hopkins, "Wreck of the Deutschland," in *Poems and Prose*, 24.
20. Emily Dickinson, "The Chariot," in *Favorite Poems of Emily Dickinson* (New York: Avenel Books, 1978), 138.

ELEVEN
Homeward

1. Bernard J.F. Lonergan, *Method in Theology* (New York: Seabury Press, 1972), 103, 105.
2. See William Shakespeare, Sonnet 87, lines 102, found in *The Sonnets of William Shakespeare*. The lines read: "Farewell—thou art too dear for my possessing/And like enough thou know'st thine estimate."
3. Psalm 88:10-12, KJV, spelling modernized.

Appendix
Exercises

1. "A Pilgrimage Renews a Life: Mother and Daughter and Memory," by Eleanor Munro, *The New York Times*, Sunday, July 11, 1993, 41.
2. James 1:17, KJV, spelling modernized.

Other Books of Interest from Servant Publications

On a Hill *Too* Far Away
Getting the Cross Back in the Center of Our Lives
by John Fischer

With powerful images and startling insights, *On a Hill* Too *Far Away* vividly reminds us of the glorious truths of the gospel, truths which many of us have forgotten.

We have forgotten: why the cross is the best thing that ever happened to us, how the cross forever changes the way we live, and the power and meaning of sacrifice.

On a Hill Too *Far Away* rekindles our desire and longing for the cross. It restores our vision of the incredible grace which transforms our lives and reshapes our culture. It is a call to remember the most spectacular truth of all: incredible Sundays always follow Good Fridays. *$8.99*

Finding Friendship with God
by Floyd McClung

From the moment each of us came into this world, God has wanted to count us among his closest friends. Our destiny is to have an intimate relationship with him. Why then do so many Christians feel thwarted in their efforts to get close to God?

Floyd McClung reveals the barriers that prevent Christians from enjoying God and teaches them how to talk with him, to rely on his friendship every day, to listen to him, and to grow in understanding him. *Finding Friendship with God* whets our appetite for this most intimate and satisfying love relationship. *$8.99*